www.EffortlessMath.com

... So Much More Online!

✓ FREE Math lessons

✓ More Math learning books!

✓ Mathematics Worksheets

✓ Online Math Tutors

Need a PDF version of this book?

Please visit www.EffortlessMath.com

HiSET Math Study Guide 2022 - 2023

Step-By-Step Guide to Preparing for the HiSET Math Test

By

Reza Nazari

All inquiries should be addressed to:

info@effortlessMath.com

www.EffortlessMath.com

ISBN: 978-1-63719-020-3

Published by: **Effortless Math Education Inc.**

For Online Math Practice Visit www.EffortlessMath.com

Welcome to

HiSET Math Prep
2022

Thank you for choosing Effortless Math for your HiSET Math test preparation and congratulations on making the decision to take the HiSET test! It's a remarkable move you are taking, one that shouldn't be diminished in any capacity.

That's why you need to use every tool possible to ensure you succeed on the test with the highest possible score, and this extensive study guide is one such tool.

If math has never been a strong subject for you, **don't worry**! This book will help you prepare for (and even ACE) the HiSET test's math section. As test day draws nearer, effective preparation becomes increasingly more important. Thankfully, you have this comprehensive study guide to help you get ready for the test. With this guide, you can feel confident that you will be more than ready for the HiSET Math test when the time comes.

First and foremost, it is important to note that this book is a study guide and not a textbook. It is best read from cover to cover. Every lesson of this "self-guided math book" was carefully developed to ensure that you are making the most effective use of your time while preparing for the test. This up-to-date guide reflects the 2022 test guidelines and will put you on the right track to hone your math skills, overcome exam anxiety, and boost your confidence, so that you can have your best to succeed on the HiSET Math test.

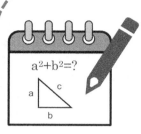

This study guide will:

☑ Explain the format of the HiSET Math test.

☑ Describe specific test-taking strategies that you can use on the test.

☑ Provide HiSET Math test-taking tips.

☑ Review all HiSET Math concepts and topics you will be tested on.

☑ Help you identify the areas in which you need to concentrate your study time.

☑ Offer exercises that help you develop the basic math skills you will learn in each section.

☑ Give **2 realistic and full-length practice tests** (featuring new question types) with detailed answers to help you measure your exam readiness and build confidence.

This resource contains everything you will ever need to succeed on the HiSET Math test. You'll get in-depth instructions on every math topic as well as tips and techniques on how to answer each question type. You'll also get plenty of practice questions to boost your test-taking confidence.

In addition, in the following pages you'll find:

➢ **How to Use This Book Effectively** – This section provides you with step-by-step instructions on how to get the most out of this comprehensive study guide.

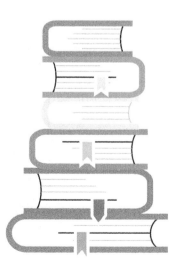

➢ **How to study for the HiSET Math Test** – A six-step study program has been developed to help you make the best use of this book and prepare for your HiSET Math test. Here you'll find tips and strategies to guide your study program and help you understand HiSET Math and how to ace the test.

➤ **HiSET Math Review** – Learn everything you need to know about the HiSET Math test.

➤ **HiSET Math Test-Taking Strategies** – Learn how to effectively put these recommended test-taking techniques into use for improving your HiSET Math score.

➤ **Test Day Tips** – Review these tips to make sure you will do your best when the big day comes.

Effortless Math's HiSET Online Center

Effortless Math Online HiSET Center offers a complete study program, including the following:

✓ Step-by-step instructions on how to prepare for the HiSET Math test

✓ Numerous HiSET Math worksheets to help you measure your math skills

✓ Complete list of HiSET Math formulas

✓ Video lessons for all HiSET Math topics

✓ Full-length HiSET Math practice tests

✓ And much more...

No Registration Required.

Visit **EffortlessMath.com/HiSET** to find your online HiSET Math resources.

How to Use This Book Effectively

L ook no further when you need a study guide to improve your math skills to succeed on the math portion of the HiSET test. Each chapter of this comprehensive guide to the HiSET Math will provide you with the knowledge, tools, and understanding needed for every topic covered on the test.

It's imperative that you understand each topic before moving onto another one, as that's the way to guarantee your success. Each chapter provides you with examples and a step-by-step guide of every concept to better understand the content that will be on the test. To get the best possible results from this book:

➢ **Begin studying long before your test date**. This provides you ample time to learn the different math concepts. The earlier you begin studying for the test, the sharper your skills will be. Do not procrastinate! Provide yourself with plenty of time to learn the concepts and feel comfortable that you understand them when your test date arrives.

➢ **Practice consistently**. Study HiSET Math concepts at least 20 to 30 minutes a day. Remember, slow and steady wins the race, which can be applied to preparing for the HiSET Math test. Instead of cramming to tackle everything at once, be patient and learn the math topics in short bursts.

➢ Whenever you get a math problem wrong, **mark it off, and review it later** to make sure you understand the concept.

➢ Start each session by **looking over the previous material.**

➢ Once you've reviewed the book's lessons, **take the practice tests at the back of the book** to gauge your level of readiness. Then, review your results. Read detailed answers and solutions for each question you missed.

➢ **Take another practice test** to get an idea of how ready you are to take the actual exam. Taking the practice tests will give you the confidence you need on test day. Simulate the HiSET testing environment by sitting in a quiet room free from distraction. Make sure to clock yourself with a timer.

How to Study for the HiSET Math Test

S tudying for the HiSET Math test can be a really daunting and boring task. What's the best way to go about it? Is there a certain study method that works better than others? Well, studying for the HiSET Math can be done effectively. The following six-step program has been designed to make preparing for the HiSET Math test more efficient and less overwhelming.

Step **1** - Create a study plan
Step **2** - Choose your study resources
Step **3** - Review, Learn, Practice
Step **4** - Learn and practice test-taking strategies
Step **5** - Learn the HiSET Test format and take practice tests
Step **6** - Analyze your performance

STEP 1: Create a Study Plan

It's always easier to get things done when you have a plan. Creating a study plan for the HiSET Math test can help you to stay on track with your studies. It's important to sit down and prepare a study plan with what works with your life, work, and any other obligations you may have. Devote enough time each day to studying. It's also a great idea to break down  each section of the exam into blocks and study one concept at a time.

It's important to understand that there is no "right" way to create a study plan. Your study plan will be personalized based on your specific needs and learning style.

Follow these guidelines to create an effective study plan for your HiSET Math test:

★ **Analyze your learning style and study habits** – Everyone has a different learning style. It is essential to embrace your individuality and the unique way you learn. Think about what works and what doesn't work for you. Do you prefer HiSET Math prep books or a combination of textbooks and video lessons? Does it work better for you if you study every

night for thirty minutes or is it more effective to study in the morning before going to work?

★ **Evaluate your schedule** – Review your current schedule and find out how much time you can consistently devote to HiSET Math study.

★ **Develop a schedule** – Now it's time to add your study schedule to your calendar like any other obligation. Schedule time for study, practice, and review. Plan out which topic you will study on which day to ensure that you're devoting enough time to each concept. Develop a study plan that is mindful, realistic, and flexible.

★ **Stick to your schedule** – A study plan is only effective when it is followed consistently. You should try to develop a study plan that you can follow for the length of your study program.

★ **Evaluate your study plan and adjust as needed** – Sometimes you need to adjust your plan when you have new commitments. Check in with yourself regularly to make sure that you're not falling behind in your study plan. Remember, the most important thing is sticking to your plan. Your study plan is all about helping you be more productive. If you find that your study plan is not as effective as you want, don't get discouraged. It's okay to make changes as you figure out what works best for you.

STEP 2: Choose Your Study Resources

There are numerous textbooks and online resources available for the HiSET Math test, and it may not be clear where to begin. Don't worry! This study guide provides everything you need to fully prepare for your HiSET Math test. In addition to the book content, you can also use Effortless Math's online resources. (video lessons, worksheets, formulas, etc.) On each page, there is

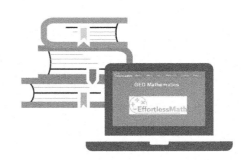

a link (and a QR code) to an online webpage which provides a comprehensive review of the topic, step-by-step instruction, video tutorial, and numerous examples and exercises to help you fully understand the concept.

You can also visit EffortlessMath.com/HiSET to find your online HiSET Math resources.

STEP 3: Review, Learn, Practice

This HiSET Math study guide breaks down each subject into specific skills or content areas. For instance, the percent concept is separated into different topics—percent calculation, percent increase and decrease, percent problems, etc. Use this book to help you go over all key math concepts and topics on the HiSET Math test.

As you read each topic, take notes or highlight the concepts you would like to go over again in the future. If you're unfamiliar with a topic or something is difficult for you, use the link (or the QR code) at the bottom of the page to find the webpage that provides more instruction about that topic. For each math topic, plenty of instructions, step-by-step guides, and examples are provided to ensure you get a good grasp of the material.

Quickly review the topics you do understand to get a brush-up of the material. Be sure to do the practice questions provided at the end of every chapter to measure your understanding of the concepts.

STEP 4: Learn and Practice Test-taking Strategies

In the following sections, you will find important test-taking strategies and tips that can help you earn extra points. You'll learn how to think strategically and when to guess if you don't know the answer to a question. Using HiSET Math test-taking strategies and tips can help you raise your score and do well on the test. Apply test taking strategies on the practice tests to help you boost your confidence.

STEP 5: Learn the HiSET Test Format and Take Practice Tests

The *HiSET Test Review* section provides information about the structure of the HiSET test. Read this section to learn more about the HiSET test structure, different test sections, the number of questions in each section, and the section time limits. When you have a prior understanding of the test format and different types of HiSET Math questions, you'll feel more confident when you take the actual exam.

Once you have read through the instructions and lessons and feel like you are ready to go – take advantage of both of the full-length HiSET Math practice tests available in this study guide. Use the practice tests to sharpen your skills and build confidence.

The HiSET Math practice tests offered at the end of the book are formatted similarly to the actual HiSET Math test. When you take each practice test, try to simulate actual testing conditions. To take the practice tests, sit in a quiet space, time yourself, and work through as many of the questions as time allows. The practice tests are followed by detailed answer explanations to help you find your weak areas, learn from your mistakes, and raise your HiSET Math score.

STEP 6: Analyze Your Performance

After taking the practice tests, look over the answer keys and explanations to learn which questions you answered correctly and which you did not. Never be discouraged if you make a few mistakes. See them as a learning opportunity. This will highlight your strengths and weaknesses.

You can use the results to determine if you need additional practice or if you are ready to take the actual HiSET Math test.

Looking for more?

Visit EffortlessMath.com/HiSET to find hundreds of HiSET Math worksheets, video tutorials, practice tests, HiSET Math formulas, and much more.

Or scan this QR code.

No Registration Required.

HiSET Test Review

T he High School Equivalency Test (HiSET), commonly known as HiSET, is a standardized test and was released in the year 2014. This test was created by the ITP (Iowa Testing Programs) and ETS (Educational Testing Service). The HiSET is equal to the HiSET test. Currently, there are twelve states that offer the HiSET®: California, Iowa, Louisiana, Maine, Massachusetts, Missouri, Montana, Nevada, New Hampshire, New Jersey, Tennessee, and Wyoming.

HiSET test takers can choose to take the test using a computer, or with pencil and paper.

The HiSET is made up of five distinct sections:

- Social Studies,
- Language Arts Reading
- Language Arts Writing
- Science
- Mathematics

The HiSET Mathematics test is a 90-minute, single-section test that covers basic mathematics topics, quantitative problem-solving and algebraic questions. There are approximately 50-55 Multiple-choice questions on Mathematics section. Calculator is allowed in the Math section.

HiSET Math Test-Taking Strategies

Here are some test-taking strategies that you can use to maximize your performance and results on the HiSET Math test.

#1 : USE THIS APPROACH TO ANSWER EVERY HiSET MATH QUESTION

- Review the question to identify keywords and important information.

- Translate the keywords into math operations so you can solve the problem.

- Review the answer choices. What are the differences between answer choices?

- Draw or label a diagram if needed.

- Try to find patterns.

- Find the right method to answer the question. Use straightforward math, plug in numbers, or test the answer choices (backsolving).

- Double-check your work.

#2 : USE EDUCATED GUESSING

This approach is applicable to the problems you understand to some degree but cannot solve using straightforward math. In such cases, try to filter out as many answer choices as possible before picking an answer. In cases where you don't have a clue about what a certain problem entails, don't waste any time trying to eliminate answer choices. Just choose one randomly before moving onto the next question.

As you can ascertain, direct solutions are the most optimal approach. Carefully read through the question, determine what the solution is using the math you have learned before, then coordinate the answer with one of the choices available to you. Are you stumped? Make your best guess, then move on.

Don't leave any fields empty! Even if you're unable to work out a problem, strive to answer it. Take a guess if you have to. You will not lose points by getting an answer wrong, though you may gain a point by getting it correct!

#3 : BALLPARK

A ballpark answer is a rough approximation. When we become overwhelmed by calculations and figures, we end up making silly mistakes. A decimal that is moved by one unit can change an answer from right to wrong, regardless of the number of steps that you went through to get it. That's where ballparking can play a big part.

If you think you know what the correct answer may be (even if it's just a ballpark answer), you'll usually have the ability to eliminate a couple of choices. While answer choices are usually based on the average student error and/or values that are closely tied, you will still be able to weed out choices that are way far afield. Try to find answers that aren't in the proverbial ballpark when you're looking for a wrong answer on a multiple-choice question. This is an optimal approach to eliminating answers to a problem.

#4 : BACKSOLVING

All questions on the HiSET Math test will be in multiple-choice format. Many test-takers prefer multiple-choice questions, as at least the answer is right there. You'll typically have five answers to pick from. You simply need to figure out which one is correct. Usually, the best way to go about doing so is "backsolving."

As mentioned earlier, direct solutions are the most optimal approach to answering a question. Carefully read through a problem, calculate a solution, then correspond the answer with one of the choices displayed in front of you. If you can't calculate a solution, your next best approach involves "backsolving."

When backsolving a problem, contrast one of your answer options against the problem you are asked, then see which of them is most relevant. More often than not, answer choices are listed in ascending or descending order. In such cases, try out the choices B or C. If it's not correct, you can go either down or up from there.

#5 : PLUGGING IN NUMBERS

"Plugging in numbers" is a strategy that can be applied to a wide range of different math problems on the HiSET Math test. This approach is typically used to simplify a challenging question so that it is more understandable. By using the strategy carefully, you can find the answer without too much trouble.

The concept is fairly straightforward–replace unknown variables in a problem with certain values. When selecting a number, consider the following:

- Choose a number that's basic (just not too basic). Generally, you should avoid choosing 1 (or even 0). A decent choice is 2.

- Try not to choose a number that is displayed in the problem.

- Make sure you keep your numbers different if you need to choose at least two of them.

- More often than not, choosing numbers merely lets you filter out some of your answer choices. As such, don't just go with the first choice that gives you the right answer.

- If several answers seem correct, then you'll need to choose another value and try again. This time, though, you'll just need to check choices that haven't been eliminated yet.

- If your question contains fractions, then a potential right answer may involve either an LCD (least common denominator) or an LCD multiple.

- 100 is the number you should choose when you are dealing with problems involving percentages.

HiSET Math – Test Day Tips

After practicing and reviewing all the math concepts you've been taught, and taking some HiSET mathematics practice tests, you'll be prepared for test day. Consider the following tips to be extra-ready come test time.

Before Your Test

What to do the night before:

■ **Relax!** One day before your test, study lightly or skip studying altogether. You shouldn't attempt to learn something new, either. There are plenty of reasons why studying the evening before a big test can work against you. Put it this way— a marathoner wouldn't go out for a sprint before the day of a big race. Mental marathoners–such as yourself–should not study for any more than one hour 24 hours before a HiSET test. That's because your brain requires some rest to be at its best. The night before your exam, spend some time with family or friends, or read a book.

■ **Avoid bright screens** - You'll have to get some good shuteye the night before your test. Bright screens (such as the ones coming from your laptop, TV, or mobile device) should be avoided altogether. Staring at such a screen will keep your brain up, making it hard to drift asleep at a reasonable hour.

■ **Make sure your dinner is healthy** - The meal that you have for dinner should be nutritious. Be sure to drink plenty of water as well. Load up on your complex carbohydrates, much like a marathon runner would do. Pasta, rice, and potatoes are ideal options here, as are vegetables and protein sources.

■ **Get your bag ready for test day** - The night prior to your test, pack your bag with your stationery, admissions pass, ID, and any other gear that you need. Keep the bag right by your front door.

■ **Make plans to reach the testing site** - Before going to sleep, ensure that you understand precisely how you will arrive at the site of the test. If parking is something you'll have to find first, plan for it. If you're dependent on public transit, then review the schedule. You should also make sure that the train/bus/subway/streetcar you use will be running. Find out about road closures as well. If a parent or friend is accompanying you, ensure that they understand what steps they have to take as well.

The Day of the Test

- **Get up reasonably early, but not too early.**

- **Have breakfast** - Breakfast improves your concentration, memory, and mood. As such, make sure the breakfast that you eat in the morning is healthy. The last thing you want to be is distracted by a grumbling tummy. If it's not your own stomach making those noises, another test taker close to you might be instead. Prevent discomfort or embarrassment by consuming a healthy breakfast. Bring a snack with you if you think you'll need it.

- **Follow your daily routine** - Do you watch Good Morning America each morning while getting ready for the day? Don't break your usual habits on the day of the test. Likewise, if coffee isn't something you drink in the morning, then don't take up the habit hours before your test. Routine consistency lets you concentrate on the main objective—doing the best you can on your test.

- **Wear layers** - Dress yourself up in comfortable layers. You should be ready for any kind of internal temperature. If it gets too warm during the test, take a layer off.

- **Get there on time** - The last thing you want to do is get to the test site late. Rather, you should be there 45 minutes prior to the start of the test. Upon your arrival, try not to hang out with anybody who is nervous. Any anxious energy they exhibit shouldn't influence you.

- **Leave the books at home** - No books should be brought to the test site. If you start developing anxiety before the test, books could encourage you to do some last-minute studying, which will only hinder you. Keep the books far away—better yet, leave them at home.

- **Make your voice heard** - If something is off, speak to a proctor. If medical attention is needed or if you'll require anything, consult the proctor prior to the start of the test. Any doubts you have should be clarified. You should be entering the test site with a state of mind that is completely clear.

■ **Have faith in yourself** - When you feel confident, you will be able to perform at your best. When you are waiting for the test to begin, envision yourself receiving an outstanding result. Try to see yourself as someone who knows all the answers, no matter what the questions are. A lot of athletes tend to use this technique–particularly before a big competition. Your expectations will be reflected by your performance.

During your test

■ **Be calm and breathe deeply** - You need to relax before the test, and some deep breathing will go a long way to help you do that. Be confident and calm. You got this. Everybody feels a little stressed out just before an evaluation of any kind is set to begin. Learn some effective breathing exercises. Spend a minute meditating before the test starts. Filter out any negative thoughts you have. Exhibit confidence when having such thoughts.

■ **Concentrate on the test** - Refrain from comparing yourself to anyone else. You shouldn't be distracted by the people near you or random noise. Concentrate exclusively on the test. If you find yourself irritated by surrounding noises, earplugs can be used to block sounds off close to you. Don't forget–the test is going to last several hours if you're taking more than one subject of the test. Some of that time will be dedicated to brief sections. Concentrate on the specific section you are working on during a particular moment. Do not let your mind wander off to upcoming or previous sections.

■ **Skip challenging questions** - Optimize your time when taking the test. Lingering on a single question for too long will work against you. If you don't know what the answer is to a certain question, use your best guess, and mark the question so you can review it later on. There is no need to spend time attempting to solve something you aren't sure about. That time would be better served handling the questions you can actually answer well. You will not be penalized for getting the wrong answer on a test like this.

■ **Try to answer each question individually** - Focus only on the question you are working on. Use one of the test-taking strategies to solve the problem. If you aren't able to come up with an answer, don't get frustrated. Simply skip that question, then move onto the next one.

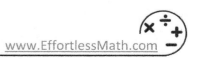

- **Don't forget to breathe!** Whenever you notice your mind wandering, your stress levels boosting, or frustration brewing, take a thirty-second break. Shut your eyes, drop your pencil, breathe deeply, and let your shoulders relax. You will end up being more productive when you allow yourself to relax for a moment.

- **Review your answer.** If you still have time at the end of the test, don't waste it. Go back and check over your answers. It is worth going through the test from start to finish to ensure that you didn't make a sloppy mistake somewhere.

- **Optimize your breaks** - When break time comes, use the restroom, have a snack, and reactivate your energy for the subsequent section. Doing some stretches can help stimulate your blood flow.

After your test

- **Take it easy** - You will need to set some time aside to relax and decompress once the test has concluded. There is no need to stress yourself out about what you could've said, or what you may have done wrong. At this point, there's nothing you can do about it. Your energy and time would be better spent on something that will bring you happiness for the remainder of your day.

- **Redoing the test** - Did you pass the test? Congratulations! Your hard work paid off! Passing this test means that you are now as knowledgeable as somebody who has graduated high school.

  If you have failed your test, though, don't worry! The test can be retaken. In such cases, you will need to follow the retake policy established by your state. You also need to re-register to take the exam again.

Contents

Simplifying Fractions 2

Adding and Subtracting Fractions 4

Multiplying and Dividing Fractions 6

Adding Mixed Numbers 8

Subtracting Mixed Numbers 10

Multiplying Mixed Numbers 12

Dividing Mixed Numbers 14

Comparing Decimals 16

Rounding Decimals 18

Adding and Subtracting Decimals 20

Multiplying and Dividing Decimals 22

Adding and Subtracting Integers 24

Multiplying and Dividing Integers 26

Order of Operation 28

Integers and Absolute Value 30

Simplifying Ratios 32

Proportional Ratios 34

Create Proportion 36

Similarity and Ratios 38

Percent Problems 40

Percent of Increase and Decrease 42

Discount, Tax and Tip 44

Simple Interest 46

Simplifying Variable Expressions 48

Simplifying Polynomial Expressions 50

Evaluating One Variable 52

Evaluating Two Variables 54

The Distributive Property 56

One–Step Equations 58

Multi –Step Equations 60

System of Equations 62

Graphing Single–Variable Inequalities 64

One–Step Inequalities 66

Multi –Step Inequalities 68

Finding Slope 70

Graphing Lines Using Slope–Intercept Form 72

Writing Linear Equations 74

Finding Midpoint 76

Finding Distance of Two Points 78

Multiplication Property of Exponents 80

Division Property of Exponents 82

Powers of Products and Quotients 84

Zero and Negative Exponents 86

Negative Exponents and Negative Bases 88

Scientific Notation 90

Radicals 92

Simplifying Polynomials 94

Adding and Subtracting Polynomials 96

Multiplying Binomials 98

Multiplying and Dividing Monomials 100

Multiplying a Polynomial and a Monomial 102

Multiplying Monomials 104

Multiplying Monomials- Answers 105

Factoring Trinomials 106

The Pythagorean Theorem 108

Triangles 110

Polygons 112

Circles 114

Cubes 116

Trapezoids 118

Rectangular Prisms...120

Cylinder 122

Mean, Median, Mode, and Range of the Given Data 124

Probability Problems...126

Pie Graph...128

Permutations and Combinations 130

Function Notation and Evaluation 132

Adding and Subtracting Functions 134

Multiplying and Dividing Functions.....................................136

Composition of Functions 138

Time to test 140

HiSET Mathematics Practice Test 1......................................142

HiSET Mathematics Practice Test 2......................................160

HiSET Mathematics Practice Tests Answer Keys..................178

HiSET Mathematics Practice Test 1 Explanations 179

HiSET Mathematics Practice Test 2 explanations 189

Topic	Simplifying Fractions
Notes	✓ Evenly divide both the top and bottom of the fraction by $2, 3, 5, 7, \ldots$ etc. ✓ Continue until you can't go any further.
Example	***Simplify*** $\frac{36}{48}$ To simplify $\frac{36}{48}$, find a number that both 36 and 48 are divisible by. Both are divisible by 12. Then: $\frac{36}{48} = \frac{36 \div 12}{48 \div 12} = \frac{3}{4}$

Your Turn!	1) $\frac{3}{15} =$	2) $\frac{11}{55} =$
	3) $\frac{12}{48} =$	4) $\frac{11}{99} =$
	5) $\frac{15}{75} =$	6) $\frac{25}{100} =$
	7) $\frac{16}{72} =$	8) $\frac{32}{96} =$
Find more at bit.ly/3nOGNko	9) $\frac{15}{65} =$	10) $\frac{48}{92} =$

Topic	Simplifying Fractions – Answers
Notes	✓ Evenly divide both the top and bottom of the fraction by $2, 3, 5, 7, ...$ etc. ✓ Continue until you can't go any further.
Example	**Simplify** $\frac{36}{48}$ To simplify $\frac{36}{48}$, find a number that both 36 and 48 are divisible by. Both are divisible by 12. Then: $\frac{36}{48} = \frac{36 \div 12}{48 \div 12} = \frac{3}{4}$

Your Turn!		
	1) $\frac{3}{15} = \frac{1}{5}$	2) $\frac{11}{55} = \frac{1}{5}$
	3) $\frac{12}{48} = \frac{1}{4}$	4) $\frac{11}{99} = \frac{1}{9}$
	5) $\frac{15}{75} = \frac{1}{5}$	6) $\frac{25}{100} = \frac{1}{4}$
	7) $\frac{16}{72} = \frac{2}{9}$	8) $\frac{32}{96} = \frac{1}{3}$
	9) $\frac{15}{65} = \frac{3}{13}$	10) $\frac{48}{92} = \frac{12}{23}$

Find more at

bit.ly/3nOGNko

Topic	**Adding and Subtracting Fractions**
Notes	✓ For "like" fractions (fractions with the same denominator), add or subtract the numerators and write the answer over the common denominator. ✓ Find equivalent fractions with the same denominator before you can add or subtract fractions with different denominators. ✓ Adding and Subtracting with the same denominator: $$\frac{a}{b} + \frac{c}{b} = \frac{a+c}{b} \ , \frac{a}{b} - \frac{c}{b} = \frac{a-c}{b}$$ ✓ Adding and Subtracting fractions with different denominators: $$\frac{a}{b} + \frac{c}{d} = \frac{ad+bc}{bd} , \frac{a}{b} - \frac{c}{d} = \frac{ad-bc}{bd}$$
Example	*Find the sum.* $\frac{3}{5} + \frac{2}{3} = \frac{(3)3+(5)(2)}{5 \times 3} = \frac{19}{15}$ *Subtract.* $\frac{4}{7} - \frac{3}{7} = \frac{1}{7}$
Your Turn! **Find more at** bit.ly/3nKet2X	1) $\frac{2}{3} + \frac{1}{5} =$ 2) $\frac{8}{7} - \frac{3}{5} =$ 3) $\frac{4}{9} + \frac{5}{8} =$ 4) $\frac{5}{8} - \frac{2}{5} =$ 5) $\frac{2}{5} + \frac{1}{6} =$ 6) $\frac{2}{3} - \frac{1}{4} =$ 7) $\frac{8}{9} + \frac{5}{7} =$ 8) $\frac{6}{7} - \frac{5}{9} =$

Topic	Adding and Subtracting Fractions - Answers
Notes	✓ For "like" fractions (fractions with the same denominator), add or subtract the numerators and write the answer over the common denominator. ✓ Find equivalent fractions with the same denominator before you can add or subtract fractions with different denominators. ✓ Adding and Subtracting with the same denominator: $$\frac{a}{b} + \frac{c}{b} = \frac{a+c}{b}, \quad \frac{a}{b} - \frac{c}{b} = \frac{a-c}{b}$$ ✓ Adding and Subtracting fractions with different denominators: $$\frac{a}{b} + \frac{c}{d} = \frac{ad+bc}{bd}, \frac{a}{b} - \frac{c}{d} = \frac{ad-bc}{bd}$$
Example	***Find the sum.*** $\frac{3}{5} + \frac{2}{3} = \frac{(3)3+(5)(2)}{5 \times 3} = \frac{19}{15}$ ***Subtract.*** $\frac{4}{7} - \frac{3}{7} = \frac{1}{7}$
Your Turn! **Find more at** bit.ly/3nKet2X	1) $\frac{2}{3} + \frac{1}{5} = \frac{13}{15}$ 2) $\frac{8}{7} - \frac{3}{5} = \frac{19}{35}$ 3) $\frac{4}{9} + \frac{5}{8} = \frac{77}{72}$ 4) $\frac{5}{8} - \frac{2}{5} = \frac{9}{40}$ 5) $\frac{2}{5} + \frac{1}{6} = \frac{17}{30}$ 6) $\frac{2}{3} - \frac{1}{4} = \frac{5}{12}$ 7) $\frac{8}{9} + \frac{5}{7} = \frac{101}{63}$ 8) $\frac{6}{7} - \frac{5}{9} = \frac{19}{63}$

Topic	**Multiplying and Dividing Fractions**
Notes	✓ Multiplying fractions: multiply the top numbers and multiply the bottom numbers. ✓ Dividing fractions: Keep, Change, Flip Keep first fraction, change division sign to multiplication, and flip the numerator and denominator of the second fraction. Then, solve!
Examples	*Multiply.* $\frac{2}{5} \times \frac{3}{4} =$ Multiply the top numbers and multiply the bottom numbers. $\frac{2}{5} \times \frac{3}{4} = \frac{2\times3}{5\times4} = \frac{6}{20}$, simplify: $\frac{6}{20} = \frac{6\div2}{20\div2} = \frac{3}{10}$ *Divide.* $\frac{2}{5} \div \frac{3}{4} =$ Keep first fraction, change division sign to multiplication, and flip the numerator and denominator of the second fraction. Then: $\frac{2}{5} \div \frac{3}{4} = \frac{2}{5} \times \frac{4}{3} = \frac{2\times4}{5\times3} = \frac{8}{15}$
Your Turn! **Find more at** bit.ly/3haSiQW	1) $\frac{3}{8} \times \frac{2}{5} =$ 2) $\frac{4}{9} \div \frac{3}{4} =$ 3) $\frac{2}{7} \times \frac{3}{5} =$ 4) $\frac{2}{5} \div \frac{7}{12} =$ 5) $\frac{1}{7} \times \frac{4}{9} =$ 6) $\frac{2}{9} \div \frac{3}{7} =$ 7) $\frac{4}{7} \times \frac{3}{8} =$ 8) $\frac{1}{6} \div \frac{3}{4} =$

Topic	**Multiplying and Dividing Fractions - Answers**
Notes	✓ Multiplying fractions: multiply the top numbers and multiply the bottom numbers. ✓ Dividing fractions: Keep, Change, Flip Keep first fraction, change division sign to multiplication, and flip the numerator and denominator of the second fraction. Then, solve!
Examples	**Multiply.** $\frac{2}{5} \times \frac{3}{4} =$ Multiply the top numbers and multiply the bottom numbers. $\frac{2}{5} \times \frac{3}{4} = \frac{2 \times 3}{5 \times 4} = \frac{6}{20}$, simplify: $\frac{6}{20} = \frac{6 \div 2}{20 \div 2} = \frac{3}{10}$ **Divide.** $\frac{2}{5} \div \frac{3}{4} =$ Keep first fraction, change division sign to multiplication, and flip the numerator and denominator of the second fraction. Then: $\frac{2}{5} \div \frac{3}{4} = \frac{2}{5} \times \frac{4}{3} = \frac{2 \times 4}{5 \times 3} = \frac{8}{15}$

Your Turn!		
	1) $\frac{3}{8} \times \frac{2}{5} = \frac{3}{20}$	2) $\frac{4}{9} \div \frac{3}{4} = \frac{16}{27}$
	3) $\frac{2}{7} \times \frac{3}{5} = \frac{6}{35}$	4) $\frac{2}{5} \div \frac{7}{12} = \frac{24}{35}$
	5) $\frac{1}{7} \times \frac{4}{9} = \frac{4}{63}$	6) $\frac{2}{9} \div \frac{3}{7} = \frac{14}{27}$
Find more at bit.ly/3haSiQW	7) $\frac{4}{7} \times \frac{3}{8} = \frac{3}{14}$	8) $\frac{1}{6} \div \frac{3}{4} = \frac{2}{9}$

Topic	**Adding Mixed Numbers**

Notes	Use the following steps for adding mixed numbers.
	
	  ✓ Add whole numbers of the mixed numbers.
	  ✓ Add the fractions of each mixed number.
	  ✓ Find the Least Common Denominator (LCD) if necessary.
	  ✓ Add whole numbers and fractions.
	  ✓ Write your answer in lowest terms.

Example	***Add mixed numbers.*** $1\frac{1}{2} + 2\frac{2}{3} =$ Rewriting our equation with parts separated, $1 + \frac{1}{2} + 2 + \frac{2}{3}$ Add whole numbers: $1 + 2 = 3$ Add fractions: $\frac{1}{2} + \frac{2}{3} = \frac{3}{6} + \frac{4}{6} = \frac{7}{6} = 1\frac{1}{6}$, Now, combine the whole and fraction parts: $3 + 1 + \frac{1}{6} = 4\frac{1}{6}$

Your Turn!		
	1) $2\frac{1}{15} + 1\frac{2}{5} =$	2) $1\frac{3}{10} + 3\frac{1}{5} =$
	3) $1\frac{1}{10} + 2\frac{2}{5} =$	4) $2\frac{5}{6} + 2\frac{2}{9} =$
	5) $2\frac{2}{7} + 1\frac{2}{21} =$	6) $1\frac{3}{8} + 3\frac{2}{3} =$
	7) $1\frac{1}{6} + 4\frac{2}{7} =$	8) $2\frac{1}{6} + 1\frac{2}{5} =$

Find more at

bit.ly/2M4oAB

Topic	Adding Mixed Numbers - Answers
Notes	Use the following steps for adding mixed numbers. ✓ Add whole numbers of the mixed numbers. ✓ Add the fractions of each mixed number. ✓ Find the Least Common Denominator (LCD) if necessary. ✓ Add whole numbers and fractions. ✓ Write your answer in lowest terms.
Example	***Add mixed numbers.*** $1\frac{1}{2} + 2\frac{2}{3} =$ Rewriting our equation with parts separated, $1 + \frac{1}{2} + 2 + \frac{2}{3}$ Add whole numbers: $1 + 2 = 3$ Add fractions: $\frac{1}{2} + \frac{2}{3} = \frac{3}{6} + \frac{4}{6} = \frac{7}{6} = 1\frac{1}{6}$ Now, combine the whole and fraction parts: $3 + 1 + \frac{1}{6} = 4\frac{1}{6}$

Your Turn!

1) $2\frac{1}{15} + 1\frac{2}{5} = 3\frac{7}{15}$ 2) $1\frac{3}{10} + 3\frac{1}{5} = 4\frac{1}{2}$

3) $1\frac{1}{10} + 2\frac{2}{5} = 3\frac{1}{2}$ 4) $2\frac{5}{6} + 2\frac{2}{9} = 5\frac{1}{18}$

5) $2\frac{2}{7} + 1\frac{2}{21} = 3\frac{8}{21}$ 6) $1\frac{3}{8} + 3\frac{2}{3} = 5\frac{1}{24}$

Find more at

bit.ly/2M4oABB

7) $1\frac{1}{6} + 4\frac{2}{7} = 5\frac{19}{42}$ 8) $2\frac{1}{6} + 1\frac{2}{5} = 3\frac{17}{30}$

Topic	**Subtracting Mixed Numbers**
Notes	Use the following steps for subtracting mixed numbers. ✓ Convert mixed numbers into improper fractions. $a\frac{c}{b} = \frac{ab+c}{b}$ ✓ Find equivalent fractions with the same denominator for unlike fractions (fractions with different denominators) ✓ Subtract the second fraction from the first one. ✓ Write your answer in lowest terms and convert it into a mixed number if the answer is an improper fraction.
Example	***Subtract.*** $5\frac{1}{2} - 2\frac{2}{3} =$ Convert mixed numbers into fractions: $5\frac{1}{2} = \frac{5\times2+1}{2} = \frac{11}{2}$ and $2\frac{2}{3} = \frac{2\times3+2}{3} = \frac{8}{3}$, these two fractions are "unlike" fractions. (they have different denominators). Find equivalent fractions with the same denominator. Use this formula: $\frac{a}{b} - \frac{c}{d} = \frac{ad-bc}{bd}$ $\frac{11}{2} - \frac{8}{3} = \frac{(11)(3)-(2)(8)}{2\times3} = \frac{33-16}{6} = \frac{17}{6}$, the answer is an improper fraction, convert it into a mixed number. $\frac{17}{6} = 2\frac{5}{6}$
Your Turn!	1) $3\frac{1}{4} - 1\frac{2}{3} =$ 2) $4\frac{4}{9} - 1\frac{1}{3} =$
	3) $6\frac{1}{4} - 1\frac{2}{7} =$ 4) $8\frac{2}{3} - 1\frac{1}{4} =$
Find more at bit.ly/3aD3KDG	5) $8\frac{3}{4} - 1\frac{3}{8} =$ 6) $2\frac{3}{8} - 1\frac{2}{3} =$
	7) $8\frac{3}{5} - 1\frac{2}{25} =$ 8) $5\frac{2}{3} - 2\frac{4}{7} =$

Topic	**Subtracting Mixed Numbers - Answers**
Notes	Use the following steps for subtracting mixed numbers. ✓ Convert mixed numbers into improper fractions. $a\frac{c}{b} = \frac{ab+c}{b}$ ✓ Find equivalent fractions with the same denominator for unlike fractions (fractions with different denominators) ✓ Subtract the second fraction from the first one. ✓ Write your answer in lowest terms and convert it into a mixed number if the answer is an improper fraction.
Example	***Subtract.*** $5\frac{1}{2} - 2\frac{2}{3} =$ Convert mixed numbers into fractions: $5\frac{1}{2} = \frac{5\times2+1}{2} = \frac{11}{2}$ and $2\frac{2}{3} = \frac{2\times3+2}{3} = \frac{8}{3}$, these two fractions are "unlike" fractions. (they have different denominators). Find equivalent fractions with the same denominator. Use this formula: $\frac{a}{b} - \frac{c}{d} = \frac{ad-bc}{bd}$ $\frac{11}{2} - \frac{8}{3} = \frac{(11)(3)-(2)(8)}{2\times3} = \frac{33-16}{6} = \frac{17}{6}$, the answer is an improper fraction, convert it into a mixed number. $\frac{17}{6} = 2\frac{5}{6}$

Your Turn!	1) $3\frac{1}{4} - 1\frac{2}{3} = 1\frac{7}{12}$	2) $4\frac{4}{9} - 1\frac{1}{3} = 3\frac{1}{9}$
	3) $6\frac{1}{4} - 1\frac{2}{7} = 4\frac{27}{28}$	4) $8\frac{2}{3} - 1\frac{1}{4} = 7\frac{5}{12}$
Find more at bit.ly/3aD3KDG 	5) $8\frac{3}{4} - 1\frac{3}{8} = 7\frac{3}{8}$	6) $2\frac{3}{8} - 1\frac{2}{3} = \frac{17}{24}$
	7) $8\frac{3}{5} - 1\frac{2}{25} = 7\frac{13}{25}$	8) $5\frac{2}{3} - 2\frac{4}{7} = 3\frac{2}{21}$

Topic	**Multiplying Mixed Numbers**
Notes	✓ Convert the mixed numbers into fractions. $a\dfrac{c}{b} = a + \dfrac{c}{b} = \dfrac{ab+c}{b}$ ✓ Multiply fractions and simplify if necessary. $\dfrac{a}{b} \times \dfrac{c}{d} = \dfrac{a \times c}{b \times d}$ ✓ If the answer is an improper fraction (numerator is bigger than denominator), convert it into a mixed number.
Example	***Multiply*** $2\dfrac{1}{4} \times 3\dfrac{1}{2}$ Convert mixed numbers into fractions: $2\dfrac{1}{4} = \dfrac{2 \times 4 + 1}{4} = \dfrac{9}{4}$ and $3\dfrac{1}{2} = \dfrac{3 \times 2 + 1}{2} = \dfrac{7}{2}$ Multiply two fractions: $\dfrac{9}{4} \times \dfrac{7}{2} = \dfrac{9 \times 7}{4 \times 2} = \dfrac{63}{8}$ The answer is an improper fraction. Convert it into a mixed number: $$\dfrac{63}{8} = 7\dfrac{7}{8}$$

Your Turn!	1) $3\dfrac{1}{3} \times 4\dfrac{1}{8} =$	2) $5\dfrac{1}{2} \times 2\dfrac{6}{7} =$
	3) $3\dfrac{1}{3} \times 3\dfrac{3}{4} =$	4) $2\dfrac{2}{9} \times 6\dfrac{1}{3} =$
	5) $2\dfrac{2}{7} \times 4\dfrac{3}{5} =$	6) $1\dfrac{4}{7} \times 9\dfrac{1}{2} =$
Find more at bit.ly/3aPy7XJ	7) $3\dfrac{3}{5} \times 4\dfrac{1}{3} =$	8) $5\dfrac{1}{4} \times 1\dfrac{1}{7} =$

Topic	**Multiplying Mixed Numbers - Answers**
Notes	✓ Convert the mixed numbers into fractions. $a\dfrac{c}{b} = a + \dfrac{c}{b} = \dfrac{ab+c}{b}$ ✓ Multiply fractions and simplify if necessary. $\dfrac{a}{b} \times \dfrac{c}{d} = \dfrac{a \times c}{b \times d}$ ✓ If the answer is an improper fraction (numerator is bigger than denominator), convert it into a mixed number.
Example	**Multiply** $2\dfrac{1}{4} \times 3\dfrac{1}{2}$ Convert mixed numbers into fractions: $2\dfrac{1}{4} = \dfrac{2\times4+1}{4} = \dfrac{9}{4}$ and $3\dfrac{1}{2} = \dfrac{3\times2+1}{2} = \dfrac{7}{2}$ Multiply two fractions: $\dfrac{9}{4} \times \dfrac{7}{2} = \dfrac{9\times7}{4\times2} = \dfrac{63}{8}$ The answer is an improper fraction. Convert it into a mixed number: $$\dfrac{63}{8} = 7\dfrac{7}{8}$$
Your Turn! **Find more at** bit.ly/3aPy7XJ	1) $3\dfrac{1}{3} \times 4\dfrac{1}{8} = 13\dfrac{3}{4}$ 2) $5\dfrac{1}{2} \times 2\dfrac{6}{7} = 15\dfrac{5}{7}$ 3) $3\dfrac{1}{3} \times 3\dfrac{3}{4} = 12\dfrac{1}{2}$ 4) $2\dfrac{2}{9} \times 6\dfrac{1}{3} = 14\dfrac{2}{27}$ 5) $2\dfrac{2}{7} \times 4\dfrac{3}{5} = 10\dfrac{18}{35}$ 6) $1\dfrac{4}{7} \times 9\dfrac{1}{2} = 14\dfrac{13}{14}$ 7) $3\dfrac{3}{5} \times 4\dfrac{1}{3} = 15\dfrac{3}{5}$ 8) $5\dfrac{1}{4} \times 1\dfrac{1}{7} = 6$

Topic	Dividing Mixed Numbers
Notes	✓ Convert the mixed numbers into improper fractions. $$a\frac{c}{b} = a + \frac{c}{b} = \frac{ab+c}{b}$$ ✓ Divide fractions and simplify if necessary.
Example	*Solve.* $2\frac{1}{3} \div 1\frac{1}{4} =$ Converting mixed numbers to fractions: $2\frac{1}{3} \div 1\frac{1}{4} = \frac{7}{3} \div \frac{5}{4}$ Keep, Change, Flip: $\frac{7}{3} \div \frac{5}{4} = \frac{7}{3} \times \frac{4}{5} = \frac{7 \times 4}{3 \times 5} = \frac{28}{15} = 1\frac{13}{15}$

Your Turn!		
	1) $2\frac{4}{7} \div 1\frac{1}{5} =$	2) $3\frac{3}{10} \div 2\frac{5}{8} =$
	3) $4\frac{2}{3} \div 3\frac{2}{5} =$	4) $5\frac{4}{5} \div 4\frac{3}{4} =$
	5) $1\frac{8}{9} \div 2\frac{3}{7} =$	6) $3\frac{3}{8} \div 2\frac{2}{5} =$
	7) $4\frac{1}{5} \div 3\frac{1}{9} =$	8) $4\frac{2}{3} \div 1\frac{8}{9} =$
	9) $4\frac{1}{6} \div 3\frac{2}{3} =$	10) $6\frac{1}{3} \div 4\frac{1}{6} =$

Find more at

bit.ly/2KLPk9k

Topic	Dividing Mixed Numbers- Answers
Notes	✓ Convert the mixed numbers into improper fractions. $$a\frac{c}{b} = a + \frac{c}{b} = \frac{ab + c}{b}$$ ✓ Divide fractions and simplify if necessary.
Example	***Solve.*** $2\frac{1}{3} \div 1\frac{1}{4} =$ Converting mixed numbers to fractions: $2\frac{1}{3} \div 1\frac{1}{4} = \frac{7}{3} \div \frac{5}{4}$ Keep, Change, Flip: $\frac{7}{3} \div \frac{5}{4} = \frac{7}{3} \times \frac{4}{5} = \frac{7\times4}{3\times5} = \frac{28}{15} = 1\frac{13}{15}$

Your Turn!		
	1) $2\frac{4}{7} \div 1\frac{1}{5} = 2\frac{1}{7}$	2) $3\frac{3}{10} \div 2\frac{5}{8} = 1\frac{9}{35}$
	3) $4\frac{2}{3} \div 3\frac{2}{5} = 1\frac{19}{51}$	4) $5\frac{4}{5} \div 4\frac{3}{4} = 1\frac{21}{95}$
	5) $1\frac{8}{9} \div 2\frac{3}{7} = \frac{7}{9}$	6) $3\frac{3}{8} \div 2\frac{2}{5} = 1\frac{13}{32}$
	7) $4\frac{1}{5} \div 3\frac{1}{9} = 1\frac{7}{20}$	8) $4\frac{2}{3} \div 1\frac{8}{9} = 2\frac{8}{17}$

Find more at

bit.ly/2KLPk9k

9) $4\frac{1}{6} \div 3\frac{2}{3} = 1\frac{3}{22}$	10) $6\frac{1}{3} \div 4\frac{1}{6} = 1\frac{13}{25}$

Topic	**Comparing Decimals**	
Notes	Decimals: is a fraction written in a special form. For example, instead of writing $\frac{1}{2}$ you can write 0.5. For comparing decimals: ✓ Compare each digit of two decimals in the same place value. ✓ Start from left. Compare hundreds, tens, ones, tenth, hundredth, etc. ✓ To compare numbers, use these symbols: - Equal to $=$, Less than $<$, Greater than $>$ Greater than or equal $\geq$, Less than or equal $\leq$	
Examples	***Compare 0.40 and 0.04.*** 0.40 *is greater than* 0.04, because the tenth place of 0.40 is 4, but the tenth place of 0.04 is zero. Then: $0.40 > 0.04$ ***Compare 0.0912 and 0.912.*** 0.912 *is greater than* 0.0912, because the tenth place of 0.912 is 9, but the tenth place of 0.0912 is zero. Then: $0.0912 < 0.912$	
Your Turn! **Find more at** bit.ly/2WHt2Za	1) $0.32 \square 0.36$	2) $1.68 \square 1.70$
	3) $19.1 \square 19.09$	4) $2.45 \square 2.089$
	5) $1.258 \square 12.58$	6) $0.89 \square 0.890$
	7) $2.657 \square 3.568$	8) $0.368 \square 0.683$

Topic	**Comparing Decimals – Answers**
Notes	Decimals: is a fraction written in a special form. For example, instead of writing $\frac{1}{2}$ you can write 0.5. For comparing decimals: ✓ Compare each digit of two decimals in the same place value. ✓ Start from left. Compare hundreds, tens, ones, tenth, hundredth, etc. ✓ To compare numbers, use these symbols: - Equal to $=$, Less than $<$, Greater than $>$ Greater than or equal $\geq$, Less than or equal $\leq$
Examples	*Compare 0.40 and 0.04.* 0.40 *is greater than* 0.04, because the tenth place of 0.40 is 4, but the tenth place of 0.04 is zero. Then: $0.40 > 0.04$ *Compare 0.0912 and 0.912.* 0.912 *is greater than* 0.0912, because the tenth place of 0.912 is 9, but the tenth place of 0.0912 is zero. Then: $0.0912 < 0.912$

Your Turn!		
	1) $0.32 < 0.36$	2) $1.68 < 1.70$
	3) $19.1 > 19.09$	4) $2.45 > 2.089$
	5) $1.258 < 12.58$	6) $0.89 = 0.890$
Find more at bit.ly/2WHt2Za	7) $2.657 < 3.568$	8) $0.368 < 0.683$

Topic	**Rounding Decimals**
Notes	✓ We can round decimals to a certain accuracy or number of decimal places. ✓ Let's review place values: For example: 35.4817 3: tens 5: ones 4: tenths 8: hundredths 1: thousandths 7: tens thousandths ✓ To round a decimal, find the place value you'll round to. ✓ Find the digit to the right of the place value you're rounding to. If it is 5 or bigger, add 1 to the place value you're rounding to and remove all digits on its right side. If the digit to the right of the place value is less than 5, keep the place value and remove all digits on the right.
Example	**Round 12.8365 to the hundredth place value.** First look at the next place value to the right, (thousandths). It's 6 and it is greater than 5. Thus add 1 to the digit in the hundredth place. It is 3. → $3 + 1 = 4$, then, the answer is 12.84
Your Turn! **Find more at** bit.ly/3mKEluf	***Round each number to the underlined place value.*** 1) 23.5<u>6</u>3 = 2) 1.2<u>2</u>3 = 3) 55.<u>4</u>23 = 4) 2<u>5</u>.62 = 5) 11.<u>2</u>65 = 6) 33.5<u>0</u>5 = 7) 4.4<u>8</u>3 = 8) 9.0<u>1</u>8 =

Topic	Rounding Decimals – Answers
Notes	✓ We can round decimals to a certain accuracy or number of decimal places. ✓ Let's review place values: For example: 35.4817 3: tens 5: ones 4: tenths 8: hundredths 1: thousandths 7:tens thousandths ✓ To round a decimal, find the place value you'll round to. ✓ Find the digit to the right of the place value you're rounding to. If it is 5 or bigger, add 1 to the place value you're rounding to and remove all digits on its right side. If the digit to the right of the place value is less than 5, keep the place value and remove all digits on the right.
Example	*Round 12.8365 to the hundredth place value.* First look at the next place value to the right, (thousandths). It's 6 and it is greater than 5. Thus add 1 to the digit in the hundredth place. It is 3. → $3 + 1 = 4$, then, the answer is 12.84
Your Turn!	*Round each number to the underlined place value.*

1) 23.5<u>6</u>3= 23.56	2) 1.2<u>2</u>3= 1.22
3) 55.<u>4</u>23 = 55.4	4) 2<u>5</u>.62 = 26
5) 11.<u>2</u>65 = 11.3	6) 33.5<u>0</u>5 = 33.51
7) 4.4<u>8</u>3= 4.48	8) 9.0<u>1</u>8= 9.02

Find more at

bit.ly/3mKEluf

Topic	**Adding and Subtracting Decimals**
Notes	✓ Line up the numbers. ✓ Add zeros to have same number of digits for both numbers if necessary. ✓ Add or subtract using column addition or subtraction.
Examples	***Add***. $2.6 + 5.33 =$ First line up the numbers: $\begin{array}{r} 2.6 \\ +\,5.33 \\ \hline \end{array}$ →Add zeros to have same number of digits for both numbers. $\begin{array}{r} 2.60 \\ +\,5.33 \\ \hline \end{array}$ → Start with the hundredths place. $0 + 3 = 3$, $\begin{array}{r} 2.60 \\ +\,5.33 \\ \hline 3 \end{array}$ → Continue with tenths place. $6 + 3 = 9$, $\begin{array}{r} 2.60 \\ +\,5.33 \\ \hline .93 \end{array}$ → Add the ones place. $2 + 5 = 7$, $\begin{array}{r} 2.60 \\ +\,5.33 \\ \hline 7.93 \end{array}$ ***Subtract***. $4.79 - 3.13 =$ $\begin{array}{r} 4.79 \\ -\,3.13 \\ \hline \end{array}$ Start with the hundredths place. $9 - 3 = 6$, $\begin{array}{r} 4.79 \\ -\,3.13 \\ \hline 6 \end{array}$, continue with tenths place. $7 - 1 = 6$, $\begin{array}{r} 4.79 \\ -\,3.13 \\ \hline .66 \end{array}$, subtract the ones place. $4 - 3 = 1$, $\begin{array}{r} 4.79 \\ -\,3.13 \\ \hline 1.66 \end{array}$
Your Turn! **Find more at** bit.ly/38uyUdx	1) $28.15 + 16.58 =$ 2) $65.36 - 56.16 =$ 3) $38.19 + 24.18 =$ 4) $57.26 - 43.54 =$ 5) $21.67 + 37.91 =$ 6) $39.58 - 26.44 =$

Topic	Adding and Subtracting Decimals - Answers
Notes	✓ Line up the numbers. ✓ Add zeros to have same number of digits for both numbers if necessary. ✓ Add or subtract using column addition or subtraction.
Examples	**Add.** $2.6 + 5.33 =$ First line up the numbers: $\begin{array}{r} 2.6 \\ +\,5.33 \\ \hline \end{array}$ → Add zeros to have same number of digits for both numbers. $\begin{array}{r} 2.60 \\ +\,5.33 \\ \hline \end{array}$ → Start with the hundredths place. $0 + 3 = 3$, $\begin{array}{r} 2.60 \\ +\,5.33 \\ \hline 3 \end{array}$ → Continue with tenths place. $6 + 3 = 9$, $\begin{array}{r} 2.60 \\ +\,5.33 \\ \hline .93 \end{array}$ → Add the ones place. $2 + 5 = 7$, $\begin{array}{r} 2.60 \\ +\,5.33 \\ \hline 7.93 \end{array}$ **Subtract.** $4.79 - 3.13 = \begin{array}{r} 4.79 \\ -\,3.13 \\ \hline \end{array}$ Start with the hundredths place. $9 - 3 = 6$, $\begin{array}{r} 4.79 \\ -\,3.13 \\ \hline 6 \end{array}$, continue with tenths place. $7 - 1 = 6$, $\begin{array}{r} 4.79 \\ -\,3.13 \\ \hline .66 \end{array}$, subtract the ones place. $4 - 3 = 1$, $\begin{array}{r} 4.79 \\ -\,3.13 \\ \hline 1.66 \end{array}$

Your Turn! **Find more at** bit.ly/38uyUdx	1) $28.15 + 16.58 = 44.73$	2) $65.36 - 56.16 = 9.20$
	3) $38.19 + 24.18 = 62.37$	4) $57.26 - 43.54 = 13.72$
	5) $21.67 + 37.91 = 59.58$	6) $39.58 - 26.44 = 13.14$

Topic	**Multiplying and Dividing Decimals**
Notes	For Multiplication: ✓ Ignore the decimal point and set up and multiply the numbers as you do with whole numbers. ✓ Count the total number of decimal places in both factors. ✓ Place the decimal point in the product. For Division: ✓ If the divisor is not a whole number, move decimal point to right to make it a whole number. Do the same for dividend. ✓ Divide similar to whole numbers.
Examples	*Find the product*. $1.2 \times 2.3 =$ Set up and multiply the numbers as you do with whole numbers. Line up the numbers: $\begin{smallmatrix}12\\ \times 23\end{smallmatrix}$ → Multiply: $\begin{smallmatrix}12\\ \times 23\\ \hline 276\end{smallmatrix}$ → Count the total number of decimal places in both of the factors. There are two decimal digits. Then: $1.2 \times 2.3 = 2.76$ *Find the quotient*. $5.6 \div 0.8 =$ The divisor is not a whole number. Multiply it by 10 to get 8. → $0.8 \times 10 = 8$ Do the same for the dividend to get 56 → $5.6 \times 10 = 56$ Now, divide: $56 \div 8 = 7$. The answer is 7.
Your Turn! **Find more at** bit.ly/34DZ0cS	1) $1.16 \times 0.5 =$ 2) $45.5 \div 5 =$ 3) $0.9 \times 0.68 =$ 4) $66.8 \div 0.2 =$ 5) $0.16 \times 0.4 =$ 6) $58.9 \div 100 =$

Topic	Multiplying and Dividing Decimals – Answers
Notes	For Multiplication: ✓ Ignore the decimal point and set up and multiply the numbers as you do with whole numbers. ✓ Count the total number of decimal places in both factors. ✓ Place the decimal point in the product. For Division: ✓ If the divisor is not a whole number, move decimal point to right to make it a whole number. Do the same for dividend. ✓ Divide similar to whole numbers.
Examples	***Find the product***. $1.2 \times 2.3 =$ Set up and multiply the numbers as you do with whole numbers. Line up the numbers: $\frac{\times 23}{}$ → Multiply: $\frac{\overset{12}{\times 23}}{276}$ → Count the total number of decimal places in both of the factors. There are two decimal digits. Then: $1.2 \times 2.3 = 2.76$ ***Find the quotient***. $5.6 \div 0.8 =$ The divisor is not a whole number. Multiply it by 10 to get 8. → $0.8 \times 10 = 8$ Do the same for the dividend to get $56 \to 5.6 \times 10 = 56$ Now, divide: $56 \div 8 = 7$. The answer is 7.

Your Turn! **Find more at** bit.ly/34DZ0cS 	1) $1.16 \times 0.5 = 0.58$	2) $45.5 \div 5 = 9.1$
	3) $0.9 \times 0.68 = 0.612$	4) $66.8 \div 0.2 = 334$
	5) $0.16 \times 0.4 = 0.064$	6) $58.9 \div 100 = 0.589$

Topic	Adding and Subtracting Integers
Notes	✓ Integers include: zero, counting numbers, and the negative of the counting numbers. $\{..., -3, -2, -1, 0, 1, 2, 3, ...\}$ ✓ Add a positive integer by moving to the right on the number line. ✓ Add a negative integer by moving to the left on the number line. Subtract an integer by adding its opposite.
Examples	*Solve*. $(4) - (-8) =$ Keep the first number and convert the sign of the second number to its opposite. (change subtraction into addition. Then: $(4) + 8 = 12$ *Solve*. $42 + (12 - 26) =$ First subtract the numbers in brackets, $12 - 26 = -14$ Then: $42 + (-14) = \rightarrow$ change addition into subtraction: $42 - 14 = 28$
Your Turn! **Find more at** bit.ly/3aKx5vl	1) $-(13) + 10 =$ 2) $(-6) + (-11) + 15 =$ 3) $(-13) + 7 =$ 4) $3 - (-7) + 14 =$ 5) $(-7) + (-8) =$ 6) $16 - (-4 + 8) =$ 7) $2 + (-6) + 8 =$ 8) $-(19) - (-6) + 3 =$

Topic	Adding and Subtracting Integers – Answers
Notes	✓ Integers include: zero, counting numbers, and the negative of the counting numbers. $\{\dots, -3, -2, -1, 0, 1, 2, 3, \dots\}$ ✓ Add a positive integer by moving to the right on the number line. ✓ Add a negative integer by moving to the left on the number line. Subtract an integer by adding its opposite.
Examples	***Solve***. $(4) - (-8) =$ Keep the first number and convert the sign of the second number to its opposite. (change subtraction into addition. Then: $(4) + 8 = 12$ ***Solve.*** $42 + (12 - 26) =$ First subtract the numbers in brackets, $12 - 26 = -14$ Then: $42 + (-14) = \rightarrow$ change addition into subtraction: $42 - 14 = 28$

Your Turn!		
	1) $-(13) + 10 = -3$	2) $(-6) + (-11) + 15 = -2$
	3) $(-13) + 7 = -6$	4) $3 - (-7) + 14 = 24$
Find more at bit.ly/3aKx5vI	5) $(-7) + (-8) = -15$	6) $16 - (-4 + 8) = 12$
	7) $2 + (-6) + 8 = 4$	8) $-(19) - (-6) + 3 = -10$

Topic	**Multiplying and Dividing Integers**
Notes	Use following rules for multiplying and dividing integers: ✓ (negative) × (negative) = positive ✓ (negative) ÷ (negative) = positive ✓ (negative) × (positive) = negative ✓ (negative) ÷ (positive) = negative ✓ (positive) × (positive) = positive ✓ (positive) ÷ (negative) = negative
Examples	*Solve*. $2 \times (14 - 17) =$ First subtract the numbers in brackets, $14 - 17 = -3 \rightarrow (2) \times (-3) =$ Now use this rule: (positive) × (negative) = negative $(2) \times (-3) = -6$ *Solve*. $(-7) + (-36 \div 4) =$ First divide -36 by 4 , the numbers in brackets, using this rule: (negative) ÷ (positive) = negative Then: $-36 \div 4 = -9$. Now, add -7 and -9: $(-7) + (-9) = -7 - 9 = -16$

Your Turn!	1) $(-4) \times 3 =$	2) $(-48) \div (-8) =$
	3) $(-11) \times (-3) =$	4) $81 \div (-9) =$
	5) $(15 - 12) \times (-7) =$	6) $(-12) \div (3) =$
Find more at bit.ly/3pjQW98	7) $3 \times (-7) =$	8) $(9) \div (-3) =$

Topic	**Multiplying and Dividing Integers - Answers**
Notes	Use following rules for multiplying and dividing integers: ✓ (negative) × (negative) = positive ✓ (negative) ÷ (negative) = positive ✓ (negative) × (positive) = negative ✓ (negative) ÷ (positive) = negative ✓ (positive) × (positive) = positive ✓ (positive) ÷ (negative) = negative
Examples	***Solve.*** $2 \times (14 - 17) =$ First subtract the numbers in brackets, $14 - 17 = -3 \rightarrow (2) \times (-3) =$ Now use this rule: (positive) × (negative) = negative $(2) \times (-3) = -6$ ***Solve.*** $(-7) + (-36 \div 4) =$ First divide -36 by 4, the numbers in brackets, using this rule: (negative) ÷ (positive) = negative Then: $-36 \div 4 = -9$. Now, add -7 and -9: $\qquad (-7) + (-9) = -7 - 9 = -16$

Your Turn!		
	1) $(-4) \times 3 = -12$	2) $(-48) \div (-8) = 6$
	3) $(-11) \times (-3) = 33$	4) $81 \div (-9) = -9$
	5) $(15 - 12) \times (-7) =$ -21	6) $(-12) \div (3) = -4$
Find more at bit.ly/3pjQW98	7) $3 \times (-7) = -21$	8) $(9) \div (-3) = -3$

Topic	Order of Operation
Notes	When there is more than one math operation, use PEMDAS: (to memorize this rule, remember the phrase "Please Excuse My Dear Aunt Sally") ✓ Parentheses ✓ Exponents ✓ Multiplication and Division (from left to right) ✓ Addition and Subtraction (from left to right)
Examples	***Calculate.*** $(18 - 26) \div (2^4 \div 4) =$ First simplify inside parentheses: $(-8) \div (16 \div 4) = (-8) \div (4)$ Then: $(-8) \div (4) = -2$ ***Solve.*** $(-5 \times 7) - (18 - 3^2) =$ First calculate within parentheses: $(-5 \times 7) - (18 - 3^2) = (-35) - (18 - 9)$ Then: $(-35) - (18 - 9) = -35 - 9 = -44$
Your Turn! **Find more at** bit.ly/37LBw7X	1) $(12 \times 3) \div (6 + 6) =$ 2) $(36 \div 4) + (11 - 4) =$ 3) $(-9) + (5 \times 6) + 14 =$ 4) $(-10 \times 5) \div (2^2 + 1) =$ 5) $[-16(32 \div 2^3)] \div 8 =$ 6) $(-7) + (72 \div 3^2) + 12 =$ 7) $[10(64 \div 2^4)] - 3^2 =$ 8) $3^3 + (-6 \times 2^3) + 4 =$

Topic	Order of Operation – Answers
Notes	When there is more than one math operation, use PEMDAS: (to memorize this rule, remember the phrase "Please Excuse My Dear Aunt Sally") ✓ Parentheses ✓ Exponents ✓ Multiplication and Division (from left to right) ✓ Addition and Subtraction (from left to right)
Examples	***Calculate.*** $(18 - 26) \div (2^4 \div 4) =$ First simplify inside parentheses: $(-8) \div (16 \div 4) = (-8) \div (4)$ Then: $(-8) \div (4) = -2$ ***Solve.*** $(-5 \times 7) - (18 - 3^2) =$ First calculate within parentheses: $(-5 \times 7) - (18 - 3^2) = (-35) - (18 - 9)$ Then: $(-35) - (18 - 9) = -35 - 9 = -44$

Your Turn!		
	1) $(12 \times 3) \div (6 + 6) = 3$	2) $(36 \div 4) + (11 - 4) = 16$
	3) $(-9) + (5 \times 6) + 14 = 35$	4) $(-10 \times 5) \div (2^2 + 1) = -10$
	5) $[-16(32 \div 2^3)] \div 8 = -8$	6) $(-7) + (72 \div 3^2) + 12 = 13$
	7) $[10(64 \div 2^4)] - 3^2 =$ 31	8) $3^3 + (-6 \times 2^3) + 4 = -17$

Find more at

bit.ly/37LBw7X

Topic	Integers and Absolute Value
Notes	✓ The absolute value of a number is its distance from zero, in either direction, on the number line. For example, the distance of 9 and -9 from zero on number line is 9. ✓ Absolute value is symbolized by vertical bars, as in $\lvert x \rvert$.
Example	*Calculate.* $\lvert 8 - 5 \rvert \times \lvert 12 - 16 \rvert =$ First calculate $\lvert 8 - 5 \rvert$, $\rightarrow \lvert 8 - 5 \rvert = \lvert 3 \rvert$, the absolute value of 3 is 3, $\lvert 3 \rvert = 3$ $8 \times \lvert 12 - 16 \rvert =$ Now calculate $\lvert 12 - 16 \rvert$, $\rightarrow \lvert 12 - 16 \rvert = \lvert -4 \rvert$, the absolute value of -4 is 4, $\lvert -4 \rvert = 4$. Then: $3 \times 4 = 12$

Your Turn!		
	1) $12 - \lvert 6 - 15 \rvert =$	2) $12 - \lvert 14 - 18 \rvert - \lvert 6 \rvert =$
	3) $\lvert 21 \rvert - \dfrac{\lvert -25 \rvert}{5} =$	4) $\lvert 30 \rvert + \dfrac{\lvert -49 \rvert}{7} =$
	5) $\dfrac{\lvert 7 \times -8 \rvert}{4} \times \dfrac{\lvert -12 \rvert}{2} =$	6) $\dfrac{\lvert 10 \times -6 \rvert}{5} \times \lvert -9 \rvert =$
	7) $\dfrac{\lvert -45 \rvert}{9} \times \dfrac{\lvert -42 \rvert}{7} =$	8) $\lvert -25 + 4 \rvert \times \dfrac{\lvert -8 \times 3 \rvert}{6} =$

Find more at

bit.ly/3aD521u

Topic	Integers and Absolute Value – Answers
Notes	✓ The absolute value of a number is its distance from zero, in either direction, on the number line. For example, the distance of 9 and -9 from zero on number line is 9. ✓ Absolute value is symbolized by vertical bars, as in $\lvert x \rvert$.
Example	***Calculate.*** $\lvert 8 - 5 \rvert \times \lvert 12 - 16 \rvert =$ First calculate $\lvert 8 - 5 \rvert$, $\rightarrow \lvert 8 - 5 \rvert = \lvert 3 \rvert$, the absolute value of 3 is 3, $\lvert 3 \rvert = 3$ $8 \times \lvert 12 - 16 \rvert =$ Now calculate $\lvert 12 - 16 \rvert$, $\rightarrow \lvert 12 - 16 \rvert = \lvert -4 \rvert$, the absolute value of -4 is 4, $\lvert -4 \rvert = 4$. Then: $3 \times 4 = 12$

Your Turn!		
	1) $12 - \lvert 6 - 15 \rvert = 3$	2) $12 - \lvert 14 - 18 \rvert - \lvert 6 \rvert = 2$
	3) $\lvert 21 \rvert - \dfrac{\lvert -25 \rvert}{5} = 16$	4) $\lvert 30 \rvert + \dfrac{\lvert -49 \rvert}{7} = 37$
	5) $\dfrac{\lvert 7 \times -8 \rvert}{4} \times \dfrac{\lvert -12 \rvert}{2} = 84$	6) $\dfrac{\lvert 10 \times -6 \rvert}{5} \times \lvert -9 \rvert = 108$
Find more at bit.ly/3aD521u	7) $\dfrac{\lvert -45 \rvert}{9} \times \dfrac{\lvert -42 \rvert}{7} = 30$	8) $\lvert -25 + 4 \rvert \times \dfrac{\lvert -8 \times 3 \rvert}{6} = 84$

Topic	Simplifying Ratios
Notes	✓ Ratios are used to make comparisons between two numbers. ✓ Ratios can be written as a fraction, using the word "to", or with a colon. ✓ You can calculate equivalent ratios by multiplying or dividing both sides of the ratio by the same number.
Examples	***Simplify.*** $18 : 63 =$ Both numbers 18 and 63 are divisible by $9 \Rightarrow 18 \div 9 = 2, 63 \div 9 = 7,$ Then: $18 : 63 = 2 : 7$ ***Simplify.*** $\frac{25}{45} =$ Both numbers 25 and 45 are divisible by 5, $\Rightarrow 25 \div 5 = 5, 45 \div 5 = 9,$ Then: $\frac{25}{45} = \frac{5}{9}$

Your Turn!

1) $\frac{6}{48} = \underline{\ \ }$	2) $\frac{35}{60} = \underline{\ \ }$
3) $\frac{15}{35} = \underline{\ \ }$	4) $\frac{42}{54} = \underline{\ \ }$
5) $\frac{12}{36} = \underline{\ \ }$	6) $\frac{30}{80} = \underline{\ \ }$
7) $\frac{16}{36} = \underline{\ \ }$	8) $\frac{30}{108} = \underline{\ \ }$

Find more at

bit.ly/3nKwq0Z

Topic	Simplifying Ratios – Answers
Notes	✓ Ratios are used to make comparisons between two numbers. ✓ Ratios can be written as a fraction, using the word "to", or with a colon. ✓ You can calculate equivalent ratios by multiplying or dividing both sides of the ratio by the same number.
Examples	***Simplify.*** $18:63 =$ Both numbers 18 and 63 are divisible by 9 $\Rightarrow 18 \div 9 = 2$, $63 \div 9 = 7$, Then: $18:63 = 2:7$ ***Simplify.*** $\frac{25}{45} =$ Both numbers 25 and 45 are divisible by 5, $\Rightarrow 25 \div 5 = 5$, $45 \div 5 = 9$, Then: $\frac{25}{45} = \frac{5}{9}$
Your Turn! **Find more at** bit.ly/3nKwq0Z 	1) $\frac{6}{48} = \frac{1}{8}$ 2) $\frac{35}{60} = \frac{7}{12}$ 3) $\frac{15}{35} = \frac{3}{7}$ 4) $\frac{42}{54} = \frac{7}{9}$ 5) $\frac{12}{36} = \frac{1}{3}$ 6) $\frac{30}{80} = \frac{3}{8}$ 7) $\frac{16}{36} = \frac{4}{9}$ 8) $\frac{30}{108} = \frac{5}{18}$

Topic	**Proportional Ratios**
Notes	✓ Two ratios are proportional if they represent the same relationship. ✓ A proportion means that two ratios are equal. It can be written in two ways: $$\frac{a}{b} = \frac{c}{d} \qquad\qquad a : b = c : d$$
Example	*Solve this proportion for x.* $\frac{5}{8} = \frac{35}{x}$ Use cross multiplication: $\frac{5}{8} = \frac{35}{x} \Rightarrow 5 \times x = 8 \times 35 \Rightarrow 5x = 280$ Divide to find x: $x = \frac{280}{5} \Rightarrow x = 56$
Your Turn! **Find more at** bit.ly/37GHQxp	1) $\frac{1}{3} = \frac{7}{x} \Rightarrow x =$ ____ 2) $\frac{4}{3} = \frac{20}{x} \Rightarrow x =$ ____ 3) $\frac{3}{11} = \frac{6}{x} \Rightarrow x =$ ____ 4) $\frac{12}{20} = \frac{x}{200} \Rightarrow x =$ ____ 5) $\frac{9}{12} = \frac{27}{x} \Rightarrow x =$ ____ 6) $\frac{14}{16} = \frac{x}{80} \Rightarrow x =$ ____ 7) $\frac{5}{14} = \frac{40}{x} \Rightarrow x =$ ____ 8) $\frac{8}{12} = \frac{36}{x} \Rightarrow x =$ ____

Topic	Proportional Ratios - Answers
Notes	✓ Two ratios are proportional if they represent the same relationship. ✓ A proportion means that two ratios are equal. It can be written in two ways: $$\frac{a}{b} = \frac{c}{d} \qquad a : b = c : d$$
Example	***Solve this proportion for*** x. $\frac{5}{8} = \frac{35}{x}$ Use cross multiplication: $\frac{5}{8} = \frac{35}{x} \Rightarrow 5 \times x = 8 \times 35 \Rightarrow 5x = 280$ Divide to find x: $\quad x = \frac{280}{5} \Rightarrow x = 56$

Your Turn!		
	1) $\frac{1}{3} = \frac{7}{x} \Rightarrow x = 21$	2) $\frac{4}{3} = \frac{20}{x} \Rightarrow x = 15$
	3) $\frac{3}{11} = \frac{6}{x} \Rightarrow x = 22$	4) $\frac{12}{20} = \frac{x}{200} \Rightarrow x = 120$
	5) $\frac{9}{12} = \frac{27}{x} \Rightarrow x = 36$	6) $\frac{14}{16} = \frac{x}{80} \Rightarrow x = 70$
Find more at bit.ly/37GHQxp	7) $\frac{5}{14} = \frac{40}{x} \Rightarrow x = 112$	8) $\frac{8}{12} = \frac{36}{x} \Rightarrow x = 54$

Topic	**Create Proportion**
Notes	✓ To create a proportion, simply find (or create) two equal fractions. ✓ Use cross products to solve proportions or to test whether two ratios are equal and form a proportion. $\frac{a}{b} = \frac{c}{d} \Rightarrow a \times d = c \times b$
Example	***State if this pair of ratios form a proportion.*** $\frac{2}{3}$ *and* $\frac{12}{30}$ Use cross multiplication: $\frac{2}{3} = \frac{12}{30} \rightarrow 2 \times 30 = 12 \times 3 \rightarrow 60 = 36$, which is not correct. Therefore, this pair of ratios doesn't form a proportion.

Your Turn! | ***State if each pair of ratios form a proportion.***

1) $\frac{3}{5}$ *and* $\frac{24}{45}$

2) $\frac{4}{9}$ *and* $\frac{16}{24}$

3) $\frac{3}{11}$ *and* $\frac{9}{33}$

4) $\frac{7}{10}$ *and* $\frac{14}{20}$

5) $\frac{7}{9}$ *and* $\frac{48}{81}$

6) $\frac{6}{8}$ *and* $\frac{12}{14}$

7) $\frac{2}{10}$ *and* $\frac{6}{30}$

8) $\frac{3}{18}$ *and* $\frac{19}{28}$

Find more at

bit.ly/37GHQxp

9) Solve.

Five pencils costs $0.50. How many pencils can you buy for $2.50? _____

Topic	Create Proportion – Answers
Notes	✓ To create a proportion, simply find (or create) two equal fractions. ✓ Use cross products to solve proportions or to test whether two ratios are equal and form a proportion. $\frac{a}{b} = \frac{c}{d} \Rightarrow a \times d = c \times b$
Example	*State if this pair of ratios form a proportion.* $\frac{2}{3}$ *and* $\frac{12}{30}$ Use cross multiplication: $\frac{2}{3} = \frac{12}{30} \rightarrow 2 \times 30 = 12 \times 3 \rightarrow 60 = 36$, which is not correct. Therefore, this pair of ratios doesn't form a proportion.
Your Turn!	*State if each pair of ratios form a proportion.* 1) $\frac{3}{5}$ and $\frac{24}{45}$, *No* 2) $\frac{4}{9}$ and $\frac{16}{24}$, *No* 3) $\frac{3}{11}$ and $\frac{9}{33}$, *Yes* 4) $\frac{7}{10}$ and $\frac{14}{20}$, *Yes* 5) $\frac{7}{9}$ and $\frac{48}{81}$, *No* 6) $\frac{6}{8}$ and $\frac{12}{14}$, *No* 7) $\frac{2}{10}$ and $\frac{6}{30}$, *Yes* 8) $\frac{3}{18}$ and $\frac{19}{28}$, *No*
Find more at bit.ly/37GHQxp	9) Solve. Five pencils costs \$0.50. How many pencils can you buy for \$2.50? **5 pencils**

Topic	**Similarity and Ratios**
Notes	✓ Two figures are similar if they have the same shape. ✓ Two or more figures are similar if the corresponding angles are equal, and the corresponding sides are in proportion.
Example	*Following triangles are similar. What is the value of unknown side?* **Solution:** Find the corresponding sides and write a proportion: $\frac{4}{12} = \frac{x}{9}$. Now, use cross product to solve for x: $\frac{4}{12} = \frac{x}{9} \rightarrow 4 \times 9 = 12 \times x \rightarrow 36 = 12x$. Divide both sides by 12. Then: $12x = 36 \rightarrow \frac{36}{12} = \frac{12x}{12} \rightarrow x = 3$. The missing side is 3.

Your Turn!

1)

2)

3)

4)

5)

6)

Topic	Similarity and Ratios - Answers
Notes	✓ Two figures are similar if they have the same shape. ✓ Two or more figures are similar if the corresponding angles are equal, and the corresponding sides are in proportion.
Example	***Following triangles are similar. What is the value of unknown side?*** **Solution:** Find the corresponding sides and write a proportion: $\frac{4}{12} = \frac{x}{9}$. Now, use cross product to solve for x: $\frac{4}{12} = \frac{x}{9} \rightarrow 4 \times 9 = 12 \times x \rightarrow 36 = 12x$. Divide both sides by 12. Then: $12x = 36 \rightarrow \frac{36}{12} = \frac{12x}{12} \rightarrow x = 3$. The missing side is 3.

Your Turn!

1) 10

2) 11

3) 4

4) 8

5) 10

6) 9

Find more at

bit.ly/2KKKmcV

Topic	**Percent Problems**
Notes	✓ In each percent problem, we are looking for the base, or part or the percent. ✓ Use the following equations to find each missing section. ○ Base = Part ÷ Percent ○ Part = Percent × Base ○ Percent = Part ÷ Base
Examples	**18 *is what percent of* 30?** In this problem, we are looking for the percent. Use the following equation: $Percent = Part \div Base \rightarrow Percent = 18 \div 30 = 0.6 = 60\%$ **40 *is* 20% *of what number?*** Use the following formula: $Base = Part \div Percent \rightarrow Base = 40 \div 0.20 = 200$ 40 is 20% of 200.

Your Turn!	1) What is 20 percent of 500?	2) 24 is what percent of 160?
	3) 60 is 5 percent of what number?	4) 48 is what percent of 300?
	5) 84 is 28 percent of what number?	6) 63 is what percent of 700?
Find more at bit.ly/34Gy3FL	7) 63 is 21 percent of what number?	8) 42 is what percent of 600?

Topic	Percent Problems – Answers

Notes	✓ In each percent problem, we are looking for the base, or part or the percent.
	 ✓ Use the following equations to find each missing section.
	     ○ Base = Part ÷ Percent
	     ○ Part = Percent × Base
	     ○ Percent = Part ÷ Base

Examples	**18 *is what percent of* 30?** In this problem, we are looking for the percent. Use the following equation: $Percent = Part \div Base \rightarrow Percent = 18 \div 30 = 0.6 = 60\%$ **40 *is* 20% *of what number?*** Use the following formula: $Base = Part \div Percent \rightarrow Base = 40 \div 0.20 = 200$ 40 is 20% of 200.

Your Turn!		
	1) What is 20 percent of 500? 100	2) 24 is what percent of 160? 15%
	3) 60 is 5 percent of what number? 1,200	4) 48 is what percent of 300? 16%
	5) 84 is 28 percent of what number? 300	6) 63 is what percent of 700? 9%
Find more at bit.ly/34Gy3FL	7) 63 is 21 percent of what number? 300	8) 42 is what percent of 600? 7%

Topic	Percent of Increase and Decrease

Notes	✓ Percent of change (increase or decrease) is a mathematical concept that represents the degree of change over time.
	✓ To find the percentage of increase or decrease:
	   1- New Number – Original Number
	   2- The result ÷ Original Number × 100
	
	Or use this formula: Percent of change $= \dfrac{new\ number - original\ number}{original\ number} \times 100$

Example	The price of a printer increases from \$40 to \$50. What is the percent increase? **Solution:** Percent of change $= \dfrac{new\ number - original\ number}{original\ number} \times 100 =$ $\dfrac{50-40}{40} \times 100 = 25$ The percentage increase is 25. It means that the price of the printer increased 25%.
Your Turn! **Find more at** bit.ly/3pgPQes	1) In a class, the number of students has been increased from 30 to 33. What is the percentage increase? _____ % 2) The price of gasoline rose from \$4.60 to \$4.83 in one month. By what percent did the gas price rise? _____ % 3) A shirt was originally priced at \$60.00. It went on sale for \$54.00. What was the percent that the shirt was discounted? _____ % 4) Jason got a raise, and his hourly wage increased from \$40 to \$56. What is the percent increase? _____ %

Topic	Percent of Increase and Decrease – Answers
Notes	✓ Percent of change (increase or decrease) is a mathematical concept that represents the degree of change over time. ✓ To find the percentage of increase or decrease: 1- New Number – Original Number 2- The result ÷ Original Number × 100 Or use this formula: Percent of change = $\frac{new\ number\ -\ original\ number}{original\ number} \times 100$
Example	The price of a printer increases from \$40 to \$50. What is the percent increase? **Solution:** Percent of change = $\frac{new\ number\ -\ original\ number}{original\ number} \times 100 = \frac{50\ -\ 40}{40} \times 100 = 25$ The percentage increase is 25. It means that the price of the printer increased 25%.
Your Turn! **Find more at** bit.ly/3pgPQes 	1) In a class, the number of students has been increased from 30 to 33. What is the percentage increase? 10% 2) The price of gasoline rose from \$4.60 to \$4.83 in one month. By what percent did the gas price rise? 5% 3) A shirt was originally priced at \$60.00. It went on sale for \$54.00. What was the percent that the shirt was discounted? -—10% 4) Jason got a raise, and his hourly wage increased from \$40 to \$56. What is the percent increase? 40%

Topic	Discount, Tax and Tip
Notes	✓ Discount = Multiply the regular price by the rate of discount ✓ Selling price = original price − discount ✓ To find tax, multiply the tax rate to the taxable amount (income, property value, etc.) ✓ To find tip, multiply the rate to the selling price.
Example	The original price of a table is $300 and the tax rate is 6%. What is the final price of the table? **Solution:** First find the tax amount. To find tax: Multiply the tax rate to the taxable amount. Tax rate is 6% or 0.06. Then: $0.06 \times 300 = 18$. The tax amount is $18. Final price is: $300 + $18 = $318

Your Turn!		
	1) Original price of a chair: $350 Tax: 12%, Selling price: _____	2) Original price of a computer: $600 Discount: 15%, Selling price: _____
	3) Original price of a printer: $250 Tax: 10%, Selling price: _____	4) Original price of a sofa: $620 Discount: 25%, Selling price: _____
	5) Original price of a mattress: $800 Tax: 12%, Selling price: _____	6) Original price of a book: $150 Discount: 60%, Selling price: _____
Find more at bit.lv/2Je5lo0	7) Restaurant bill: $24.00 Tip: 25%, Final amount: _____	8) Restaurant bill: $80.00 Tip: 15%, Final amount: _____

Topic	Discount, Tax and Tip – Answers
Notes	✓ Discount = Multiply the regular price by the rate of discount ✓ Selling price = original price – discount ✓ To find tax, multiply the tax rate to the taxable amount (income, property value, etc.) ✓ To find tip, multiply the rate to the selling price.
Example	*The original price of a table is $300 and the tax rate is 6%. What is the final price of the table?* **Solution:** First find the tax amount. To find tax: Multiply the tax rate to the taxable amount. Tax rate is 6% or 0.06. Then: $0.06 \times 300 = 18$. The tax amount is $18. Final price is: $300 + $18 = $318

Your Turn!		
Find more at bit.ly/2Je5lo0 	1) Original price of a chair: $350 Tax: 12%, Selling price: $392	2) Original price of a computer: $ 600 Discount: 15%, Selling price: $510
	3) Original price of a printer: $250 Tax: 10%, Selling price: $275	4) Original price of a sofa: $620 Discount: 25%, Selling price: $465
	5) Original price of a mattress: $800 Tax: 12%, Selling price: $896	6) Original price of a book: $150 Discount: 60%, Selling price: $60
	7) Restaurant bill: $24.00 Tip: 25%, Final amount: $30	8) Restaurant bill: $80.00 Tip: 15%, Final amount: $92

Topic	Simple Interest
Notes	✓ Simple Interest: The charge for borrowing money or the return for lending it. To solve a simple interest problem, use this formula: Interest = principal x rate x time $\Rightarrow$ $I = p \times r \times t$
Example	***Find simple interest for* $3,000 *investment at* 5% *for 4 years*.** **Solution:** Use Interest formula: $I = prt$ ($P = \$3,000$, r $= 5\% = 0.05$ and $t = 4$) Then: $I = 3,000 \times 0.05 \times 4 = \$600$
Your Turn! **Find more at** bit.ly/3nJli3D	1) $200 at 3% for 2 years. Simple interest: $_____$ 2) $4,200 at 4% for 5 years. Simple interest: $_____$ 3) $720 at 2% for 5 years. Simple interest: $_____$ 4) $2,200 at 8% for 4 years. Simple interest: $_____$ 5) $1,800 at 3% for 2 years. Simple interest: $_____$ 6) $530 at 4% for 5 years. Simple interest: $_____$ 7) $5,100 at 6% for 6 months. Simple interest: $_____$ 8) $960 at 5% for 3 months. Simple interest: $_____$

Topic	Simple Interest – Answers
Notes	✓ Simple Interest: The charge for borrowing money or the return for lending it. To solve a simple interest problem, use this formula: Interest = principal x rate x time $\Rightarrow$ $\boldsymbol{I = p \times r \times t}$
Example	***Find simple interest for*** $3,000$ ***investment at*** 5% ***for 4 years.*** **Solution:** Use Interest formula: $I = prt$ ($P = \$3,000$, r $= 5\% = 0.05$ and $t = 4$) Then: $I = 3,000 \times 0.05 \times 4 = \$600$

Your Turn!		
	1) $200 at 3% for 2 years. Simple interest: $12	2) $4,200 at 4% for 5 years. Simple interest: $840
	3) $720 at 2% for 5 years. Simple interest: $72	4) $2,200 at 8% for 4 years. Simple interest: $704
	5) $1,800 at 3% for 2 years. Simple interest: $108	6) $530 at 4% for 5 years. Simple interest: $106
Find more at bit.ly/3nJli3D	7) $5,100 at 6% for 6 months. Simple interest: $153	8) $960 at 5% for 3 months. Simple interest: $12

Topic	Simplifying Variable Expressions
Notes	✓ In algebra, a variable is a letter used to stand for a number. The most common letters are: $x, y, z, a, b, c, m,$ and n. ✓ Algebraic expression is an expression contains integers, variables, and the math operations such as addition, subtraction, multiplication, division, etc. ✓ In an expression, we can combine "like" terms. (values with same variable and same power)
Example	***Simplify this expression.*** $(6x + 8x + 9) =?$ Combine like terms. Then: $(6x + 8x + 9) = 14x + 9$ **(remember you cannot combine variables and numbers).**

Your Turn!	1) $6x + 4 - 7x =$	2) $5 + 3x + 2x =$
	3) $8x + 3 - 3x =$	4) $-2 - x^2 - 6x^2 =$
	5) $3 + 10x^2 + 2 =$	6) $8x^2 + 6x + 7x^2 =$
	7) $5x^2 - 12x^2 + 8x =$	8) $2x^2 - 2x - x + 5x^2 =$
Find more at bit.ly/2WFVudQ	9) $6x - (10 - 25x) =$	10) $16x - (60x - 50) =$

Topic	Simplifying Variable Expressions – Answers
Notes	✓ In algebra, a variable is a letter used to stand for a number. The most common letters are: $x, y, z, a, b, c, m, and\ n$. ✓ Algebraic expression is an expression contains integers, variables, and the math operations such as addition, subtraction, multiplication, division, etc. ✓ In an expression, we can combine "like" terms. (values with same variable and same power)
Example	Simplify this expression. $(6x + 8x + 9) =?$ Combine like terms. Then: $(6x + 8x + 9) = 14x + 9$ (remember you cannot combine variables and numbers).

Your Turn!	1) $6x + 4 - 7x =$ $-x + 4$	2) $5 + 3x + 2x =$ $5x + 5$
	3) $8x + 3 - 3x =$ $5x + 3$	4) $-2 - x^2 - 6x^2 =$ $-7x^2 - 2$
	5) $3 + 10x^2 + 2 =$ $10x^2 + 5$	6) $8x^2 + 6x + 7x^2 =$ $15x^2 + 6x$
	7) $5x^2 - 12x^2 + 8x =$ $-7x^2 + 8x$	8) $2x^2 - 2x - x + 5x^2 =$ $7x^2 - 3x$
Find more at bit.ly/2WFVudQ	9) $6x - (10 - 25x) =$ $31x - 10$	10) $16x - (60x - 50) =$ $-44x + 50$

Topic	Simplifying Polynomial Expressions
Notes	✓ In mathematics, a polynomial is an expression consisting of variables and coefficients that involves only the operations of addition, subtraction, multiplication, and non–negative integer exponents of variables. $$P(x) = a_n x^n + a_{n-1} x^{n-1} + \dots + a_2 x^2 + a_1 x + z$$
Example	***Simplify this expression.*** $(2x^2 - x^4) - (4x^4 - x^2) =$ First use distributive property: → multiply $(-)$ into $(4x^4 - x^2)$ $(2x^2 - x^4) - (4x^4 - x^2) = 2x^2 - x^4 - 4x^4 + x^2$ Then combine "like" terms: $2x^2 - x^4 - 4x^4 + x^2 = 3x^2 - 5x^4$ And write in standard form: $3x^2 - 5x^4 = -5x^4 + 3x^2$

Your Turn!	1) $(x^3 + 3x^2) - (10x + 4x^2) =$	2) $(3x^5 + 5x^3) - (6x^3 + 9x^2) =$
	3) $(12x^4 + 4x^2) - (2x^2 - 6x^4) =$	4) $14x - 3x^2 - 2(6x^2 + 6x^3) =$
	5) $(5x^3 - 3) + 5(2x^2 - 3x^3) =$	6) $(4x^3 - 2x) - 2(4x^3 - 2x^4) =$
Find more at bit.ly/2WT5gtn	7) $3(3x - 2x^3) - 4(x^3 + 5x^2) =$	8) $(4x^2 - 3x) - (4x^3 + 6x^2) =$

Topic	Simplifying Polynomial Expressions – Answers
Notes	✓ In mathematics, a polynomial is an expression consisting of variables and coefficients that involves only the operations of addition, subtraction, multiplication, and non–negative integer exponents of variables. $$P(x) = a_n x^n + a_{n-1}x^{n-1} + \ldots + a_2 x^2 + a_1 x + a_0$$
Example	***Simplify this expression.*** $(2x^2 - x^4) - (4x^4 - x^2) =$ First use distributive property: → multiply $(-)$ into $(4x^4 - x^2)$ $(2x^2 - x^4) - (4x^4 - x^2) = 2x^2 - x^4 - 4x^4 + x^2$ Then combine "like" terms: $2x^2 - x^4 - 4x^4 + x^2 = 3x^2 - 5x^4$ And write in standard form: $3x^2 - 5x^4 = -5x^4 + 3x^2$

Your Turn!	1) $(x^3 + 3x^2) - (10x + 4x^2) =$ $x^3 - x^2 - 10x$	2) $(3x^5 + 5x^3) - (6x^3 + 9x^2) =$ $3x^5 - x^3 - 9x^2$
	3) $(12x^4 + 4x^2) - (2x^2 - 6x^4) =$ $18x^4 + 2x^2$	4) $14x - 3x^2 - 2(6x^2 + 6x^3) =$ $-12x^3 - 15x^2 + 14x$
	5) $(5x^3 - 3) + 5(2x^2 - 3x^3) =$ $-10x^3 + 10x^2 - 3$	6) $(4x^3 - 2x) - 2(4x^3 - 2x^4) =$ $4x^4 - 4x^3 - 2x$
Find more at bit.ly/2WT5gtn 	7) $3(3x - 2x^3) - 4(x^3 + 5x^2) =$ $-10x^3 - 20x^2 + 9x$	8) $(4x^2 - 3x) - (4x^3 + 6x^2) =$ $-4x^3 - 2x^2 - 3x$

Topic	**Evaluating One Variable**
Notes	✓ To evaluate one variable expression, find the variable and substitute a number for that variable. ✓ Perform the arithmetic operations.
Example	***Find the value of this expression for*** $x = -3$. $-3x - 13$ **Solution:** Substitute -3 for x, then: $-3x - 13 = -3(-3) - 13 = 9 - 13 = -4$

Your Turn!	1) $x = -2 \Rightarrow 4x + 9 =$ ____	2) $x = 3 \Rightarrow 5(3x + 5) =$ ____
	3) $x = -1 \Rightarrow 6x + 4 =$ ____	4) $x = 7 \Rightarrow 6(5x + 3) =$ ____
	5) $x = 4 \Rightarrow 5(3x + 2) =$ ____	6) $x = 6 \Rightarrow 3(2x + 4) =$ ____
	7) $x = 3 \Rightarrow 7(3x + 1) =$ ____	8) $x = 8 \Rightarrow 3(3x + 7) =$ ____
Find more at bit.ly/3ppujQZ	9) $x = 8 \Rightarrow 3(x + 6) =$ ____	10) $x = 6 \Rightarrow 3(2x + 3) =$ ____

Topic	Evaluating One Variable – Answers
Notes	✓ To evaluate one variable expression, find the variable and substitute a number for that variable. ✓ Perform the arithmetic operations.
Example	*Find the value of this expression for* $x = -3$. $\quad -3x - 13$ **Solution:** Substitute -3 for x, then: $-3x - 13 = -3(-3) - 13 = 9 - 13 = -4$

Your Turn!	1) $x = -2 \Rightarrow 4x + 9 = 1$	2) $x = 3 \Rightarrow 5(3x + 5) = 70$
	3) $x = -1 \Rightarrow 6x + 4 = -2$	4) $x = 7 \Rightarrow 6(5x + 3) = 228$
	5) $x = 4 \Rightarrow 5(3x + 2) = 70$	6) $x = 6 \Rightarrow 3(2x + 4) = 48$
	7) $x = 3 \Rightarrow 7(3x + 1) = 70$	8) $x = 8 \Rightarrow 3(3x + 7) = 93$
Find more at bit.ly/3ppujQZ	9) $x = 8 \Rightarrow 3(x + 6) = 42$	10) $x = 6 \Rightarrow 3(2x + 3) = 45$

Topic	Evaluating Two Variables
Notes	✓ To evaluate an algebraic expression, substitute a number for each variable. ✓ Perform the arithmetic operations to find the value of the expression.
Example	**Evaluate this expression for** $a = 4$ **and** $b = -2$. $5a - 6b$ **Solution:** Substitute 4 for a, and -2 for b, then: $5a - 6b = 5(4) - 6(-2) = 20 + 12 = 32$

Your Turn!	1) $-3a + 5b$, $a = 3$, $b = 2$ ———	2) $4x + 2y$, $x = -1$, $y = 4$ ———
	3) $-5a + 3b$, $a = 2$, $b = -2$ ———	4) $3x - 4y$, $x = 6$, $y = 2$ ———
	5) $2z + 14 + 6k$, $z = 5$, $k = 3$ ———	6) $7a - (9 - 3b)$, $a = 1$, $b = 1$ ———
	7) $-6a + 3b$, $a = 4$, $b = 3$ ———	8) $-2a + b$, $a = 6$, $b = 9$ ———
Find more at bit.ly/2JfrzWJ	9) $5x + 3y$, $x = 2$, $y = 9$ ———	10) $z + 7 + 3k$, $z = 4$, $k = 2$ ———

Topic	Evaluating Two Variables – Answers
Notes	✓ To evaluate an algebraic expression, substitute a number for each variable. ✓ Perform the arithmetic operations to find the value of the expression.
Example	***Evaluate this expression for*** $a = 4$ ***and*** $b = -2$. $\ 5a - 6b$ **Solution:** Substitute 4 for a, and -2 for b, then: $5a - 6b = \ 5(4) - 6(-2) = 20 + 12 = 32$

Your Turn!		
	1) $-3a + 5b, \ a = 3, \ b = 2$ 1	2) $4x + 2y, \ x = -1, \ y = 4$ 4
	3) $-5a + 3b, \ a = 2, \ b = -2$ −16	4) $3x - 4y, \ x = 6, \ y = 2$ 10
	5) $2z + 14 + 6k, \ z = 5, \ k = 3$ 42	6) $7a - (9 - 3b), \ a = 1, \ b = 1$ 1
	7) $-6a + 3b, \ a = 4, \ b = 3$ −15	8) $-2a + b, \ a = 6, \ b = 9$ −3
	9) $5x + 3y, \ x = 2, \ y = 9$ 37	10) $z + 7 + 3k, \ z = 4, \ k = 2$ 17

Find more at

bit.ly/2JfrzWJ

Topic	The Distributive Property
Notes	✓ The distributive property (or the distributive property of multiplication over addition and subtraction) simplifies and solves expressions in the form of: $a(b+c)$ or $a(b-c)$ ✓ Distributive Property rule: $$a(b+c) = ab + ac$$
Example	**Simply.** $(5)(2x-8)$ **Solution:** Use Distributive Property rule: $a(b+c) = ab + ac$ $(5)(2x-8) = (5 \times 2x) + (5) \times (-8) = 10x - 40$

Your Turn!		
	1) $(-3)(2-4x) =$	2) $(3-2x)(-5)$
	3) $6(5-9x) =$	4) $10(3-5x) =$
	5) $5(6-5x) =$	6) $(-2)(-5x+3) =$
	7) $(8-9x)(5) =$	8) $(-16x+15)(-3) =$
Find more at bit.ly/38qCaXs	9) $(-6x+8)(4) =$	10) $(-12x+21)(-3) =$

Topic	The Distributive Property – Answers
Notes	✓ The distributive property (or the distributive property of multiplication over addition and subtraction) simplifies and solves expressions in the form of: $a(b + c)$ or $a(b - c)$ ✓ Distributive Property rule: $$a(b + c) = ab + ac$$
Example	***Simply.*** $(5)(2x - 8)$ **Solution:** Use Distributive Property rule: $a(b + c) = ab + ac$ $(5)(2x - 8) = (5 \times 2x) + (5) \times (-8) = 10x - 40$

Your Turn!		
	1) $(-3)(2 - 4x) = 12x - 6$	2) $(3 - 2x)(-5) = 10x - 15$
	3) $6(5 - 9x) = -54x + 30$	4) $10(3 - 5x) = -50x + 30$
	5) $5(6 - 5x) = -25x + 30$	6) $(-2)(-5x + 3) = 10x - 6$
	7) $(8 - 9x)(5) = -45x + 40$	8) $(-16x + 15)(-3) =$ $48x - 45$
	9) $(-6x + 8)(4) = -24x + 32$	10) $(-12x + 21)(-3) =$ $36x - 63$

Find more at

bit.ly/38qCaXs

Topic	One–Step Equations
Notes	✓ You only need to perform one Math operation in order to solve the one-step equations. ✓ To solve one-step equation, find the inverse (opposite) operation is being performed. ✓ The inverse operations are: 　- Addition and subtraction 　- Multiplication and division
Example	**Solve this equation.** $x + 42 = 60 \Rightarrow x = ?$ Here, the operation is addition and its inverse operation is subtraction. To solve this equation, subtract 42 from both sides of the *equation:* $x + 42 - 42 = 60 - 42$ Then simplify: $x + 42 - 42 = 60 - 42 \Rightarrow x = 18$

Your Turn!		
	1) $x - 12 = 44 \Rightarrow x = $ ____	2) $15 = 11 + x \Rightarrow x = $ ____
	3) $x - 22 = 54 \Rightarrow x = $ ____	4) $x + 14 = 24 \Rightarrow x = $ ____
	5) $4x = 24 \Rightarrow x = $ ____	6) $\frac{x}{6} = -3 \Rightarrow x = $ ____
Find more at bit.ly/37Jq0tK	7) $66 = 22x \Rightarrow x = $ ____	8) $\frac{x}{18} = 3 \Rightarrow x = $ ____

Topic	One–Step Equations – Answers
Notes	✓ You only need to perform one Math operation in order to solve the one-step equations. ✓ To solve one-step equation, find the inverse (opposite) operation is being performed. ✓ The inverse operations are: - Addition and subtraction - Multiplication and division
Example	*Solve this equation.* $x + 42 = 60 \Rightarrow x = ?$ Here, the operation is addition and its inverse operation is subtraction. To solve this equation, subtract 42 from both sides of the *equation:* $x + 42 - 42 = 60 - 42$ Then simplify: $x + 42 - 42 = 60 - 42 \Rightarrow x = 18$

Your Turn!		
	1) $x - 12 = 44 \Rightarrow x = 56$	2) $15 = 11 + x \Rightarrow x = 4$
	3) $x - 22 = 54 \Rightarrow x = 76$	4) $x + 14 = 24 \Rightarrow x = 10$
	5) $4x = 24 \Rightarrow x = 6$	6) $\frac{x}{6} = -3 \Rightarrow x = -18$
Find more at bit.ly/37Jq0tK	7) $66 = 22x \Rightarrow x = 3$	8) $\frac{x}{18} = 3 \Rightarrow x = 54$

Topic	Multi –Step Equations
Notes	✓ Combine "like" terms on one side. ✓ Bring variables to one side by adding or subtracting. ✓ Simplify using the inverse of addition or subtraction. ✓ Simplify further by using the inverse of multiplication or division. ✓ Check your solution by plugging the value of the variable into the original equation.
Example	**Solve this equation for** x. $\quad 2x - 3 = 13$ **Solution:** The inverse of subtraction is addition. Add 3 to both sides of the equation. Then: $2x - 3 = 13 \Rightarrow 2x - 3 = 13 + 3$ $\Rightarrow 2x = 16$. Now, divide both sides by 2, then: $\frac{2x}{2} = \frac{16}{2} \Rightarrow x = 8$ Now, check the solution: $x = 8 \Rightarrow 2x - 3 = 13 \Rightarrow 2(8) - 3 = 13 \Rightarrow 16 - 3 = 13 \qquad$ The answer $x = 8$ is correct.

Your Turn!		
	1) $5x - 15 = 10 \Rightarrow x =$	2) $14 - 2x = -6 + 2x \Rightarrow x =$
	3) $3(4 - 2x) = 24 \Rightarrow x =$	4) $15 + 5x = -7 - 6x \Rightarrow x =$
	5) $-2(5 + x) = 2 \Rightarrow x =$	6) $12 - 2x = -3 - 5x \Rightarrow x =$
	7) $18 = -(x - 8) \Rightarrow x =$	8) $13 - 5x = -5 - 2x \Rightarrow x =$

Find more at

bit.ly/3nQbSEB

Topic	Multi –Step Equations – Answers
Notes	✓ Combine "like" terms on one side. ✓ Bring variables to one side by adding or subtracting. ✓ Simplify using the inverse of addition or subtraction. ✓ Simplify further by using the inverse of multiplication or division. ✓ Check your solution by plugging the value of the variable into the original equation.
Example	*Solve this equation for* x. $2x - 3 = 13$ **Solution:** The inverse of subtraction is addition. Add 3 to both sides of the equation. Then: $2x - 3 = 13 \Rightarrow 2x - 3 = 13 + 3$ $\Rightarrow 2x = 16$. Now, divide both sides by 2, then: $\frac{2x}{2} = \frac{16}{2} \Rightarrow x = 8$ Now, check the solution: $x = 8 \Rightarrow 2x - 3 = 13 \Rightarrow 2(8) - 3 = 13 \Rightarrow 16 - 3 = 13$ The answer $x = 8$ is correct.

Your Turn!	1) $5x - 15 = 10 \Rightarrow x = 5$	2) $14 - 2x = -6 + 2x \Rightarrow x = 5$
	3) $3(4 - 2x) = 24 \Rightarrow x = -2$	4) $15 + 5x = -7 - 6x \Rightarrow x = -2$
Find more at bit.ly/3nObSFB	5) $-2(5 + x) = 2 \Rightarrow x = -6$	6) $12 - 2x = -3 - 5x \Rightarrow x = -5$
	7) $18 = -(x - 8) \Rightarrow x = -10$	8) $13 - 5x = -5 - 2x \Rightarrow x = 6$

Topic	System of Equations
Notes	✓ A system of equations contains two equations and two variables. For example, consider the system of equations: $x - 2y = -2, x + 2y = 10$ ✓ The easiest way to solve a system of equation is using the elimination method. The elimination method uses the addition property of equality. You can add the same value to each side of an equation. ✓ For the first equation above, you can add $x + 2y$ to the left side and 10 to the right side of the first equation: $x - 2y + (x + 2y) = -2 + 10$. Now, if you simplify, you get: $x - 2y + (x + 2y) = -2 + 10 \rightarrow 2x = 8 \rightarrow x = 4$. Now, substitute 4 for the x in the first equation: $4 - 2y = -2$. By solving this equation, $y = 3$
Example	What is the value of x and y in this system of equations? $\begin{cases} 3x - y = 7 \\ -x + 4y = 5 \end{cases}$ **Solution:** Solving System of Equations by Elimination: $\begin{array}{l} 3x - y = 7 \\ \underline{-x + 4y = 5} \end{array}$ Multiply the second equation by 3, then add it to the first equation. $\begin{array}{l} 3x - y = 7 \\ \underline{3(-x + 4y = 5)} \end{array} \Rightarrow \begin{array}{l} 3x - y = 7 \\ \underline{-3x + 12y = 15)} \end{array} \Rightarrow 11y = 22 \Rightarrow y = 2$. Now, substitute 2 for y in the first equation and solve for x. $3x - (2) = 7 \Rightarrow 3x = 9 \Rightarrow x = 3$
Your Turn! **Find more at** bit.ly/3mPGO6k	1) $-4x + 4y = 8$ $\qquad -4x + 2y = 6$ $x = \underline{\quad}$ $y = \underline{\quad}$ 2) $-5x + y = -3$ $\qquad 3x - 8y = 24$ $x = \underline{\quad}$ $y = \underline{\quad}$ 3) $y = -2$ $\qquad 4x - 3y = 8$ $x = \underline{\quad}$ $y = \underline{\quad}$ 4) $y = -3x + 5$ $\qquad 5x - 4y = -3$ $x = \underline{\quad}$ $y = \underline{\quad}$ 5) $20x - 18y = -26$ $\qquad -10x + 6y = 22$ $x = \underline{\quad}$ $y = \underline{\quad}$ 6) $-9x - 12y = 15$ $\qquad 2x - 6y = 14$ $x = \underline{\quad}$ $y = \underline{\quad}$

Topic	System of Equations- Answers
Notes	✓ A system of equations contains two equations and two variables. For example, consider the system of equations: $x - 2y = -2, x + 2y = 10$ ✓ The easiest way to solve a system of equation is using the elimination method. The elimination method uses the addition property of equality. You can add the same value to each side of an equation. ✓ For the first equation above, you can add $x + 2y$ to the left side and 10 to the right side of the first equation: $x - 2y + (x + 2y) = -2 + 10$. Now, if you simplify, you get: $x - 2y + (x + 2y) = -2 + 10 \rightarrow 2x = 8 \rightarrow x = 4$. Now, substitute 4 for the x in the first equation: $4 - 2y = -2$. By solving this equation, $y = 3$
Example	What is the value of x and y in this system of equations? $\begin{cases} 3x - y = 7 \\ -x + 4y = 5 \end{cases}$ **Solution:** Solving System of Equations by Elimination: $\begin{array}{c} 3x - y = 7 \\ \hline -x + 4y = 5 \end{array}$ Multiply the second equation by 3, then add it to the first equation. $\begin{array}{c} 3x - y = 7 \\ \underline{3(-x + 4y = 5)} \end{array} \Rightarrow \begin{array}{c} 3x - y = 7 \\ \underline{-3x + 12y = 15)} \end{array} \Rightarrow 11y = 22 \Rightarrow y = 2$. Now, substitute 2 for y in the first equation and solve for x. $3x - (2) = 7 \Rightarrow 3x = 9 \Rightarrow x = 3$

Your Turn!	1) $-4x + 4y = 8$ $-4x + 2y = 6$ $x = -1$ $y = 1$	2) $-5x + y = -3$ $3x - 8y = 24$ $x = 0$ $y = -3$
	3) $y = -2$ $4x - 3y = 8$ $x = \dfrac{1}{2}$ $y = -2$	4) $y = -3x + 5$ $5x - 4y = -3$ $x = 1$ $y = 2$
Find more at bit.ly/3mPGO6k	5) $20x - 18y = -26$ $-10x + 6y = 22$ $x = -4$ $y = -3$	6) $-9x - 12y = 15$ $2x - 6y = 14$ $x = 1$ $y = -2$

Topic	Graphing Single–Variable Inequalities
Notes	✓ An inequality compares two expressions using an inequality sign. ✓ Inequality signs are: "less than" $<$, "greater than" $>$, "less than or equal to" $\leq$, and "greater than or equal to" $\geq$. ✓ To graph a single–variable inequality, find the value of the inequality on the number line. ✓ For less than ($<$) or greater than ($>$) draw open circle on the value of the variable. If there is an equal sign too, then use filled circle. ✓ Draw an arrow to the right for greater or to the left for less than.
Example	***Draw a graph for this inequality.*** $x < 5$ **Solution:** Since, the variable is less than 5, then we need to find 5 in the number line and draw an open circle on it. Then, draw an arrow to the left. -6 -5 -4 -3 -2 -1 0 1 2 3 4 5 6
Your Turn!	1) $x < 3$ -6 -5 -4 -3 -2 -1 0 1 2 3 4 5 6 2) $x \geq -2$ -6 -5 -4 -3 -2 -1 0 1 2 3 4 5 6
	3) $x \geq -3$ -6 -5 -4 -3 -2 -1 0 1 2 3 4 5 6 4) $x \leq 6$ -6 -5 -4 -3 -2 -1 0 1 2 3 4 5 6
Find more at bit.ly/3aJ4GGo	5) $x > -6$ -6 -5 -4 -3 -2 -1 0 1 2 3 4 5 6 6) $2 > x$ -6 -5 -4 -3 -2 -1 0 1 2 3 4 5 6
	7) $-3 \leq x$ -6 -5 -4 -3 -2 -1 0 1 2 3 4 5 6 8) $x > 1$ -6 -5 -4 -3 -2 -1 0 1 2 3 4 5 6

Topic	Graphing Single–Variable Inequalities- Answers
Notes	✓ An inequality compares two expressions using an inequality sign. ✓ Inequality signs are: "less than" $<$, "greater than" $>$, "less than or equal to" $\leq$, and "greater than or equal to" $\geq$. ✓ To graph a single–variable inequality, find the value of the inequality on the number line. ✓ For less than ($<$) or greater than ($>$) draw open circle on the value of the variable. If there is an equal sign too, then use filled circle. ✓ Draw an arrow to the right for greater or to the left for less than.
Example	***Draw a graph for this inequality.*** $x < 5$ **Solution:** Since, the variable is less than 5, then we need to find 5 in the number line and draw an open circle on it. Then, draw an arrow to the left.

Your Turn!	1) $x < 3$	2) $x \geq -2$
	3) $x \geq -3$	4) $x \leq 6$
Find more at bit.ly/3aJ4GGo	5) $x > -6$	6) $2 > x$
	7) $-3 \leq x$	8) $x > 1$

Topic	**One–Step Inequalities**
Notes	✓ Inequality signs are: "less than" <, "greater than" >, "less than or equal to" ≤, and "greater than or equal to" ≥. ✓ You only need to perform one Math operation in order to solve the one-step inequalities. ✓ To solve one-step inequalities, find the inverse (opposite) operation is being performed. ✓ For dividing or multiplying both sides by negative numbers, flip the direction of the inequality sign.
Example	**Solve this inequality.** $x + 12 < 60 \Rightarrow$ _____ Here, the operation is addition and its inverse operation is subtraction. To solve this inequality, subtract 12 from both sides of the **inequality:** $x + 12 - 12 < 60 - 12$ Then simplify: $x < 48$

Your Turn!	1) $3x < -9 \Rightarrow$ _____	2) $x + 5 > 29 \Rightarrow$ _____
	3) $-3x \geq 36 \Rightarrow$ _____	4) $x - 16 \leq 4 \Rightarrow$ _____
	5) $\frac{x}{2} \geq -9 \Rightarrow$ _____	6) $48 < 6x \Rightarrow$ _____
Find more at bit.ly/3rrElgL	7) $88 \leq 22x \Rightarrow$ _____	8) $\frac{x}{6} > 8 \Rightarrow$ _____

Topic	One–Step Inequalities - Answers
Notes	✓ Inequality signs are: "less than" $<$, "greater than" $>$, "less than or equal to" $\leq$, and "greater than or equal to" $\geq$. ✓ You only need to perform one Math operation in order to solve the one-step inequalities. ✓ To solve one-step inequalities, find the inverse (opposite) operation is being performed. ✓ For dividing or multiplying both sides by negative numbers, flip the direction of the inequality sign.
Example	***Solve this inequality.*** $x + 12 < 60 \Rightarrow$ _____ Here, the operation is addition and its inverse operation is subtraction. To solve this inequality, subtract 12 from both sides of the ***inequality:*** $x + 12 - 12 < 60 - 12$ Then simplify: $x < 48$

Your Turn!	1) $3x < -9 \Rightarrow x < -3$	2) $x + 5 > 29 \Rightarrow x > 24$
	3) $-3x \geq 36 \Rightarrow x \leq -12$	4) $x - 16 \leq 4 \Rightarrow x \leq 20$
	5) $\frac{x}{2} \geq -9 \Rightarrow x \geq -18$	6) $48 < 6x \Rightarrow 8 < x$
Find more at bit.ly/3rrEIgL	7) $88 \leq 22x \Rightarrow 4 \leq x$	8) $\frac{x}{6} > 8 \Rightarrow x > 48$

Topic	**Multi –Step Inequalities**
Notes	✓ Isolate the variable. ✓ Simplify using the inverse of addition or subtraction. ✓ Simplify further by using the inverse of multiplication or division. ✓ For dividing or multiplying both sides by negative numbers, flip the direction of the inequality sign.
Example	***Solve this inequality.*** $3x + 12 \leq 21$ **Solution:** First subtract 12 from both sides: $3x + 12 - 12 \leq 21 - 12$ Then simplify: $3x + 12 - 12 \leq 21 - 12 \rightarrow 3x \leq 9$ Now divide both sides by 3: $\frac{3x}{3} \leq \frac{9}{3} \rightarrow x \leq 3$

Your Turn!		
	1) $4x + 3 < 39 \rightarrow$ _____	2) $5x - 9 \leq 6 \rightarrow$ _____
	3) $2x - 5 \leq 17 \rightarrow$ _____	4) $14 - 7x \geq -7 \rightarrow$ _____
	5) $18 - 6x \geq -6 \rightarrow$ _____	6) $2x - 18 \leq 16 \rightarrow$ _____
Find more at bit.ly/2WK1xOr	7) $9 + 6x < 45 \rightarrow$ _____	8) $7 - 4x < 19 \rightarrow$ _____

Topic	Multi –Step Inequalities – Answers
Notes	✓ Isolate the variable. ✓ Simplify using the inverse of addition or subtraction. ✓ Simplify further by using the inverse of multiplication or division. ✓ For dividing or multiplying both sides by negative numbers, flip the direction of the inequality sign.
Example	*Solve this inequality.* $3x + 12 \leq 21$ **Solution:** First subtract 12 from both sides: $3x + 12 - 12 \leq 21 - 12$ Then simplify: $3x + 12 - 12 \leq 21 - 12 \rightarrow 3x \leq 9$ Now divide both sides by 3: $\frac{3x}{3} \leq \frac{9}{3} \rightarrow x \leq 3$
Your Turn! **Find more at** bit.ly/2WK1xOr	1) $4x + 3 < 39 \rightarrow x < 9$ 2) $5x - 9 \leq 6 \rightarrow x \leq 3$ 3) $2x - 5 \leq 17 \rightarrow x \leq 11$ 4) $14 - 7x \geq -7 \rightarrow x \leq 3$ 5) $18 - 6x \geq -6 \rightarrow x \leq 4$ 6) $2x - 18 \leq 16 \rightarrow x \leq 17$ 7) $9 + 6x < 45 \rightarrow x < 6$ 8) $7 - 4x < 19 \rightarrow x > -3$

Topic	**Finding Slope**
Notes	✓ The slope of a line represents the direction of a line on the coordinate plane. ✓ A line on coordinate plane can be drawn by connecting two points. ✓ To find the slope of a line, we need two points. ✓ The slope of a line with two points A (x_1, y_1) and B (x_2, y_2) can be found by using this formula: $\frac{y_2 - y_1}{x_2 - x_1} = \frac{rise}{\text{run}}$ ✓ The equation of a line is typically written as $y = mx + b$ where m is the slope and b is the y-intercept.
Examples	*Find the slope of the line through these two points:* $(4, -12)$ *and* $(9, 8)$. **Solution:** Slope $= \frac{y_2 - y_1}{x_2 - x_1}$. Let (x_1, y_1) be $(4, -12)$ and (x_2, y_2) be $(9, 8)$. *Then:* slope $= \frac{y_2 - y_1}{x_2 - x_1} = \frac{8 - (-12)}{9 - 4} = \frac{8 + 12}{5} = \frac{20}{5} = 4$ *Find the slope of the line with equation* $y = 5x - 6$ **Solution:** when the equation of a line is written in the form of $y = mx + b$, the slope is m. In this line: $y = 5x - 6$, the slope is 5.
Your Turn! **Find more at** bit.ly/3nMJYJv	1) $(1, 3), (5, 7)$ Slope = ____	2) $(-2, 2), (0, 4)$ Slope = ____
	3) $(4, -2), (2, 4)$ Slope = ____	4) $(-4, -1), (0, 7)$ Slope = ____
	5) $y = 4x + 15$ Slope = ____	6) $y = -6x + 3$ Slope = ____

Topic	Finding Slope – Answers
Notes	✓ The slope of a line represents the direction of a line on the coordinate plane. ✓ A line on coordinate plane can be drawn by connecting two points. ✓ To find the slope of a line, we need two points. ✓ The slope of a line with two points A (x_1, y_1) and B (x_2, y_2) can be found by using this formula: $\frac{y_2 - y_1}{x_2 - x_1} = \frac{rise}{run}$ ✓ The equation of a line is typically written as $y = mx + b$ where m is the slope and b is the y-intercept.
Examples	*Find the slope of the line through these two points:* $(4, -12)$ *and* $(9, 8)$. **Solution:** Slope $= \frac{y_2 - y_1}{x_2 - x_1}$. Let (x_1, y_1) be $(4, -12)$ and (x_2, y_2) be $(9, 8)$. *Then:* slope $= \frac{y_2 - y_1}{x_2 - x_1} = \frac{8 - (-12)}{9 - 4} = \frac{8 + 12}{5} = \frac{20}{5} = 4$ *Find the slope of the line with equation* $y = 5x - 6$ **Solution:** when the equation of a line is written in the form of $y = mx + b$, the slope is m. In this line: $y = 5x - 6$, the slope is 5.

Your Turn!	1) $(1, 3), (5, 7)$ Slope $= 1$	2) $(-2, 2), (0, 4)$ Slope $= 1$
	3) $(4, -2), (2, 4)$ Slope $= -3$	4) $(-4, -1), (0, 7)$ Slope $= 2$
Find more at bit.ly/3nMJYJv	5) $y = 4x + 15$ Slope $= 4$	6) $y = 6x + 3$ Slope $= 6$

Topic	**Graphing Lines Using Slope–Intercept Form**
Notes	✓ Slope–intercept form of a line: given the slope m and the y–intercept (the intersection of the line and y-axis) b, then the equation of the line is: $$y = mx + b$$
Example	***Sketch the graph of*** $y = -2x - 1$. **Solution:** To graph this line, we need to find two points. When x is zero the value of y is -1. And when y is zero the value of x is $-\frac{1}{2}$. $x = 0 \rightarrow y = -2(0) - 1 = -1, y = 0 \rightarrow 0$ $= -2x - 1 \rightarrow x = -\frac{1}{2}$ Now, we have two points: $(0, -1)$ and $(-\frac{1}{2}, 0)$. Find the points and graph the line. Remember that the slope of the line is $-\frac{1}{2}$.
Your Turn! **Find more at** bit.ly/3hfdnJL	1) $y = -4x + 1$ 2) $y = -x - 5$

Topic	**Graphing Lines Using Slope–Intercept Form - Answers**
Notes	✓ Slope–intercept form of a line: given the slope m and the y–intercept (the intersection of the line and y-axis) b, then the equation of the line is: $$y = mx + b$$
Example	*Sketch the graph of* $y = -2x - 1$. **Solution:** To graph this line, we need to find two points. When x is zero the value of y is -1. And when y is zero the value of x is $-\frac{1}{2}$. $$x = 0 \rightarrow y = -2(0) - 1 = -1, y = 0 \rightarrow 0$$ $$= -2x - 1 \rightarrow x = -\frac{1}{2}$$ Now, we have two points: $(0, -1)$ and $(-\frac{1}{2}, 0)$. Find the points and graph the line. Remember that the slope of the line is $-\frac{1}{2}$.
Your Turn! **Find more at** bit.ly/3hfdnJL 	1) $y = -4x + 1$ 2) $y = -x - 5$

Topic	Writing Linear Equations
Notes	✓ The equation of a line: $y = mx + b$ ✓ Identify the slope. ✓ Find the y–intercept. This can be done by substituting the slope and the coordinates of a point (x, y) on the line.
Example	**Write the equation of the line through $(3, 1)$ and $(-1, 5)$.** **Solution:** $Slop = \frac{y_2 - y_1}{x_2 - x_1} = \frac{5 - 1}{-1 - 3} = \frac{4}{-4} = -1 \rightarrow m = -1$ To find the value of b, you can use either points. The answer will be the same: $y = -x + b$ $(3, 1) \rightarrow 1 = -3 + b \rightarrow b = 4$ $(-1, 5) \rightarrow 5 = -(-1) + b \rightarrow b = 4$ The equation of the line is: $y = -x + 4$

Your Turn!	1) through: $(-1, 2), (1, 4)$ $y =$	2) through: $(8, 1), (5, 4)$ $y =$
	3) through: $(5, -1), (8, 2)$ $y =$	4) through: $(-2, 4), (4, -8)$ $y =$
	5) through: $(6, -5), (-5, 6)$ $y =$	6) through: $(4, -4), (-2, 8)$ $y =$
Find more at bit.ly/3nMKcAl	7) through $(-3, 6)$, Slope: 2 $y =$	8) through $(4, 3)$, Slope: -4 $y =$

Topic	Writing Linear Equations – Answers
Notes	✓ The equation of a line: $y = mx + b$ ✓ Identify the slope. ✓ Find the y–intercept. This can be done by substituting the slope and the coordinates of a point (x, y) on the line.
Example	**Write the equation of the line through** $(3, 1)$ **and** $(-1, 5)$. **Solution:** $Slop = \frac{y_2 - y_1}{x_2 - x_1} = \frac{5 - 1}{-1 - 3} = \frac{4}{-4} = -1 \rightarrow m = -1$ To find the value of b, you can use either points. The answer will be the same: $y = -x + b$ $(3, 1) \rightarrow 1 = -3 + b \rightarrow b = 4$ $(-1, 5) \rightarrow 5 = -(-1) + b \rightarrow b = 4$ The equation of the line is: $y = -x + 4$

Your Turn!		
	1) through: $(-1, 2), (1, 4)$ $y = x + 3$	2) through: $(8, 1), (5, 4)$ $y = -x + 9$
	3) through: $(5, -1), (8, 2)$ $y = x - 6$	4) through: $(-2, 4), (4, -8)$ $y = -2x$
	5) through: $(6, -5), (-5, 6)$ $y = -x + 1$	6) through: $(4, -4), (-2, 8)$ $y = -2x + 4$
	7) through $(-3, 6)$, Slope: 2 $y = 2x + 12$	8) through $(4, 3)$, Slope: -4 $y = -4x + 19$

Find more at

bit.ly/3nMKcAl

Topic	**Finding Midpoint**
Notes	✓ The middle of a line segment is its midpoint. ✓ The Midpoint of two endpoints A (x_1, y_1) and B (x_2, y_2) can be found using this formula: $M(\frac{x_1+x_2}{2}, \frac{y_1+y_2}{2})$
Example	Find the midpoint of the line segment with the given endpoints. $(\mathbf{1}, -\mathbf{2}), (\mathbf{3}, \mathbf{6})$ **Solution:** Midpoint $= (\frac{x_1+x_2}{2}, \frac{y_1+y_2}{2}) \rightarrow (x_1, y_1) = (1, -2)$ and $(x_2, y_2) = (3, 6)$ Midpoint $= (\frac{1+3}{2}, \frac{-2+6}{2}) \rightarrow (\frac{4}{2}, \frac{4}{2}) \rightarrow M(2, 2)$
Your Turn! **Find more at** bit.ly/3nPdnTq	1) $(2, 1), (-4, 1)$ **Midpoint** $= (\_\_, \_\_)$ 2) $(6, -2), (2, 4)$ **Midpoint** $= (\_\_, \_\_)$ 3) $(-3, 4), (-5, 0)$ **Midpoint** $= (\_\_, \_\_)$ 4) $(8, 1), (-4, 5)$ **Midpoint** $= (\_\_, \_\_)$ 5) $(6, 7), (-4, 5)$ **Midpoint** $= (\_\_, \_\_)$ 6) $(2, -3), (2, 5)$ **Midpoint** $= (\_\_, \_\_)$ 7) $(7, 3), (-1, -7)$ **Midpoint** $= (\_\_, \_\_)$ 8) $(3, 9), (-1, 5)$ **Midpoint** $= (\_\_, \_\_)$ 9) $(5, 2), (-9, 0)$ **Midpoint** $= (\_\_, \_\_)$ 10) $(2, 7), (10, -9)$ **Midpoint** $= (\_\_, \_\_)$

Topic	Finding Midpoint – Answers
Notes	✓ The middle of a line segment is its midpoint. ✓ The Midpoint of two endpoints A (x_1, y_1) and B (x_2, y_2) can be found using this formula: $M(\frac{x_1+x_2}{2}, \frac{y_1+y_2}{2})$
Example	Find the midpoint of the line segment with the given endpoints. $(\mathbf{1}, -\mathbf{2}), (\mathbf{3}, \mathbf{6})$ **Solution:** Midpoint $= (\frac{x_1+x_2}{2}, \frac{y_1+y_2}{2}) \rightarrow (x_1, y_1) = (1, -2)$ and $(x_2, y_2) = (3, 6)$ Midpoint $= (\frac{1+3}{2}, \frac{-2+6}{2}) \rightarrow (\frac{4}{2}, \frac{4}{2}) \rightarrow M(2, 2)$

Your Turn!	1) $(2, 1), (-4, 1)$ **Midpoint** $= (-1, 1)$	2) $(6, -2), (2, 4)$ **Midpoint** $= (4, 1)$
	3) $(-3, 4), (-5, 0)$ **Midpoint** $= (-4, 2)$	4) $(8, 1), (-4, 5)$ **Midpoint** $= (2, 3)$
	5) $(6, 7), (-4, 5)$ **Midpoint** $= (1, 6)$	6) $(2, -3), (2, 5)$ **Midpoint** $= (2, 1)$
Find more at bit.ly/3nPdnTq	7) $(7, 3), (-1, -7)$ **Midpoint** $= (3, -2)$	8) $(3, 9), (-1, 5)$ **Midpoint** $= (1, 7)$
	9) $(5, 2), (-9, 0)$ **Midpoint** $= (-2, 1)$	10) $(2, 7), (10, -9)$ **Midpoint** $= (6, -1)$

Topic	**Finding Distance of Two Points**
Notes	✓ Use this formula to find the distance of two points A (x_1, y_1) and B (x_2, y_2): $$d = \sqrt{(x_2 - x_1)^2 + (y_2 - y_1)^2}$$
Example	*Find the distance of two points* $(-1, 5)$ and $(4, -7)$. **Solution:** *Use distance of two points formula:* $d = \sqrt{(x_2 - x_1)^2 + (y_2 - y_1)^2}$ $(x_1, y_1) = (-1, 5)$, and $(x_2, y_2) = (4, -7)$ Then: $d = \sqrt{(x_2 - x_1)^2 + (y_2 - y_1)^2} \rightarrow d = \sqrt{(4 - (-1))^2 + (-7 - 5)^2} = \sqrt{(5)^2 + (-12)^2} = \sqrt{25 + 144} = \sqrt{169} = 13$
Your Turn!	1) $(8, 2), (-6, 2)$ **Distance** = ____ 2) $(3, -4), (3, 6)$ **Distance** = ____
	3) $(-5, 10), (7, 1)$ **Distance** = ____ 4) $(8, 1), (-4, 6)$ **Distance** = ____
	5) $(-3, 6), (-4, 5)$ **Distance** = ____ 6) $(4, -1), (14, 23)$ **Distance** = ____
	7) $(3, 5), (6, 9)$ **Distance** = ____ 8) $(2, -2), (10, 4)$ **Distance** = ____

Find more at

bit.ly/2KV50Hy

Topic	Finding Distance of Two Points - Answers
Notes	✓ Use this formula to find the distance of two points A (x_1, y_1) and B (x_2, y_2): $$d = \sqrt{(x_2 - x_1)^2 + (y_2 - y_1)^2}$$
Example	**Find the distance of two points** $(-1, 5)$ and $(4, -7)$. **Solution:** *Use distance of two points formula:* $d = \sqrt{(x_2 - x_1)^2 + (y_2 - y_1)^2}$ $(x_1, y_1) = (-1, 5)$, and $(x_2, y_2) = (4, -7)$ Then: $d = \sqrt{(x_2 - x_1)^2 + (y_2 - y_1)^2} \rightarrow d = \sqrt{(4 - (-1))^2 + (-7 - 5)^2} = \sqrt{(5)^2 + (-12)^2} = \sqrt{25 + 144} = \sqrt{169} = 13$

Your Turn!	1) $(8, 2), (-6, 2)$ **Distance** $= 14$	2) $(3, -4), (3, 6)$ **Distance** $= 10$
	3) $(-5, 10), (7, 1)$ **Distance** $= 15$	4) $(8, 1), (-4, 6)$ **Distance** $= 13$
	5) $(-3, 6), (-4, 5)$ **Distance** $= \sqrt{2}$	6) $(4, -1), (14, 23)$ **Distance** $= 26$
Find more at bit.ly/2KV50Hy	7) $(3, 5), (6, 9)$ **Distance** $= 5$	8) $(2, -2), (10, 4)$ **Distance** $= 10$

Topic	**Multiplication Property of Exponents**
Notes	✓ Exponents are shorthand for repeated multiplication of the same number by itself. For example, instead of 2×2, we can write 2^2. For $3 \times 3 \times 3 \times 3$, we can write 3^4 ✓ In algebra, a variable is a letter used to stand for a number. The most common letters are: $x, y, z, a, b, c, m, and\ n$. ✓ Exponent's rules: $x^a \times x^b = x^{a+b}$, $\frac{x^a}{x^b} = x^{a-b}$ $(x^a)^b = x^{a \times b}$ $\qquad$ $(xy)^a = x^a \times y^a$ $\qquad$ $(\frac{a}{b})^c = \frac{a^c}{b^c}$
Example	*Multiply.* $4x^3 \times 2x^2$ Use Exponent's rules: $x^a \times x^b = x^{a+b} \rightarrow x^3 \times x^2 = x^{3+2} = x^5$ Then: $4x^3 \times 2x^2 = 8x^5$
Your Turn!	1) $x^2 \times 5x =$ $\qquad\qquad$ 2) $3x^4 \times x^2 =$
	3) $3x^2 \times 4x^5 =$ $\qquad\qquad$ 4) $3x^2 \times 6xy =$
	5) $3x^5y \times 5x^2y^3 =$ $\qquad\qquad$ 6) $3x^2y^2 \times 5x^2y^8 =$
	7) $5x^2y \times 5x^2y^7 =$ $\qquad\qquad$ 8) $6x^6 \times 4x^9y^4 =$
	9) $4x^2y^5 \times 6x^5y^3 =$ $\qquad\qquad$ 10) $10x^6x^2 \times 7xy^5 =$

Find more at

bit.ly/34AWHr1

Topic	Multiplication Property of Exponents - Answers
Notes	✓ Exponents are shorthand for repeated multiplication of the same number by itself. For example, instead of 2×2, we can write 2^2. For $3 \times 3 \times 3 \times 3$, we can write 3^4 ✓ In algebra, a variable is a letter used to stand for a number. The most common letters are: $x, y, z, a, b, c, m,$ and n. ✓ Exponent's rules: $x^a \times x^b = x^{a+b}$, $\frac{x^a}{x^b} = x^{a-b}$ $(x^a)^b = x^{a \times b}$ $(xy)^a = x^a \times y^a$ $(\frac{a}{b})^c = \frac{a^c}{b^c}$
Example	***Multiply.*** $4x^3 \times 2x^2$ Use Exponent's rules: $x^a \times x^b = x^{a+b} \rightarrow x^3 \times x^2 = x^{3+2} = x^5$ Then: $4x^3 \times 2x^2 = 8x^5$

Your Turn!		
Find more at bit.ly/34AWHr1	1) $x^2 \times 5x = 5x^3$	2) $3x^4 \times x^2 = 3x^6$
	3) $3x^2 \times 4x^5 = 12x^7$	4) $3x^2 \times 6xy = 18x^3 y$
	5) $3x^5 y \times 5x^2 y^3 = 15x^7 y^4$	6) $3x^2 y^2 \times 5x^2 y^8 = 15x^4 y^{10}$
	7) $5x^2 y \times 5x^2 y^7 = 25x^4 y^8$	8) $6x^6 \times 4x^9 y^4 = 24x^{15} y^4$
	9) $4x^2 y^5 \times 6x^5 y^3 = 24x^7 y^8$	10) $10x^6 x^2 \times 7xy^5 = 70x^9 y^5$

Topic	Division Property of Exponents
Notes	✓ For division of exponents use these formulas: $\frac{x^a}{x^b} = x^{a-b}$, $x \neq 0$ $\frac{x^a}{x^b} = \frac{1}{x^{b-a}}$, $x \neq 0$, $\qquad \frac{1}{x^b} = x^{-b}$
Example	*Simplify.* $\frac{6x^3y}{36x^2y^3}$ First cancel the common factor: $6 \rightarrow \frac{6x^3y}{36x^2y^3} = \frac{x^3y}{6x^2y^3}$ Use Exponent's rules: $\frac{x^a}{x^b} = x^{a-b} \rightarrow \frac{x^3}{x^2} = x^{3-2} = x^1 = x$ Then: $\frac{6x^3y}{36x^2y^3} = \frac{xy}{6y^3} \rightarrow$ now cancel the common factor: $y \rightarrow \frac{xy}{6y^3} = \frac{x}{6y^2}$

Your Turn!

1) $\dfrac{2^5}{2^2} =$

2) $\dfrac{6x}{12x^3} =$

3) $\dfrac{3x^3}{2x^5} =$

4) $\dfrac{12x^3}{14x^6} =$

5) $\dfrac{12x^3}{9y^8} =$

6) $\dfrac{25xy^4}{5x^6y^2} =$

7) $\dfrac{2x^4y^5}{7xy^2} =$

8) $\dfrac{16x^2y^8}{4x^3} =$

Find more at

bit.ly/37JAclZ

9) $\dfrac{9x^4}{12x^7y^9} =$

10) $\dfrac{14y^8x^4}{21y^2x^8} =$

Topic	**Division Property of Exponents - Answers**
Notes	✓ For division of exponents use following formulas: $\frac{x^a}{x^b} = x^{a-b}$, $x \neq 0$ $\frac{x^a}{x^b} = \frac{1}{x^{b-a}}$, $x \neq 0$, $\frac{1}{x^b} = x^{-b}$
Example	*Simplify.* $\frac{6x^3y}{36x^2y^3}$ First cancel the common factor: $6 \to \frac{6x^3y}{36x^2y^3} = \frac{x^3y}{6x^2y^3}$ Use Exponent's rules: $\frac{x^a}{x^b} = x^{a-b} \to \frac{x^3}{x^2} = x^{3-2} = x^1 = x$ Then: $\frac{6x^3y}{36x^2y^3} = \frac{xy}{6y^3} \to$ now cancel the common factor: $y \to \frac{xy}{6y^3} = \frac{x}{6y^2}$

Your Turn!		
	1) $\frac{2^5}{2^2} = 2^3$	2) $\frac{6x}{12x^3} = \frac{1}{2x^2}$
	3) $\frac{3x^3}{2x^5} = \frac{3}{2x^2}$	4) $\frac{12x^3}{14x^6} = \frac{6}{7x^3}$
	5) $\frac{12x^3}{9y^8} = \frac{4x^3}{3y^8}$	6) $\frac{25xy^4}{5x^6y^2} = \frac{5y^2}{x^5}$
	7) $\frac{2x^4y^5}{7xy^2} = \frac{2x^3y^3}{7}$	8) $\frac{16x^2y^8}{4x^3} = \frac{4y^8}{x}$
Find more at bit.ly/37JAclZ	9) $\frac{9x^4}{12x^7y^9} = \frac{3}{4x^3y^9}$	10) $\frac{14y^8x^4}{21y^2x^8} = \frac{2y^6}{3x^4}$

Topic	**Powers of Products and Quotients**
Notes	✓ For any nonzero numbers a and b and any integer x, $$(ab)^x = a^x \times b^x, \left(\frac{a}{b}\right)^c = \frac{a^c}{b^c}$$
Example	***Simplify.*** $\left(\frac{2x^3}{x}\right)^2$ First cancel the common factor: $x \rightarrow \left(\frac{2x^3}{x}\right)^2 = (2x^2)^2$ Use Exponent's rules: $(ab)^x = a^x \times b^x$ Then: $(2x^2)^2 = (2)^2(x^2)^2 = 4x^4$

Your Turn!	1) $(3x^3x^3)^3 =$	2) $(2x^3 \times 6x)^2 =$
	3) $(10x^{11}y^3)^2 =$	4) $(9x^7y^5)^2 =$
	5) $(4x^4y^6)^3 =$	6) $(3x \times 4y^3)^2 =$
Find more at bit.ly/34CgPJm	7) $\left(\frac{5x}{x^2}\right)^2 =$	8) $\left(\frac{x^4y^4}{x^2y^2}\right)^3 =$
	9) $\left(\frac{24x}{4x^6}\right)^2 =$	10) $\left(\frac{x^6}{x^4y^2}\right)^2 =$

Topic	Powers of Products and Quotients - Answers
Notes	✓ For any nonzero numbers a and b and any integer x, $$(ab)^x = a^x \times b^x, \left(\frac{a}{b}\right)^c = \frac{a^c}{b^c}$$
Example	*Simplify.* $\left(\frac{2x^3}{x}\right)^2$ First cancel the common factor: $x \rightarrow \left(\frac{2x^3}{x}\right)^2 = (2x^2)^2$ Use Exponent's rules: $(ab)^x = a^x \times b^x$ Then: $(2x^2)^2 = (2)^2(x^2)^2 = 4x^4$

Your Turn!		
	1) $(3x^3 x^3)^3 = 27x^{18}$	2) $(2x^3 \times 6x)^2 = 144x^8$
	3) $(10x^{11}y^3)^2 =$ $100x^{22}y^6$	4) $(9x^7 y^5)^2 = 81x^{14}y^{10}$
	5) $(4x^4 y^6)^3 = 64\,x^{12}y^{18}$	6) $(3x \times 4y^3)^2 = 144x^2 y^6$
Find more at bit.ly/34CgPJm	7) $\left(\frac{5x}{x^2}\right)^2 = \frac{25}{x^2}$	8) $\left(\frac{x^4 y^4}{x^2 y^2}\right)^3 = x^6 y^6$
	9) $\left(\frac{24x}{4x^6}\right)^2 = \frac{36}{x^{10}}$	10) $\left(\frac{x^6}{x^4 y^2}\right)^2 = \frac{x^4}{y^4}$

Topic	Zero and Negative Exponents
Notes	✓ A negative exponent is the reciprocal of that number with a positive exponent. $(3)^{-2} = \frac{1}{3^2}$ ✓ Zero-Exponent Rule: $a^0 = 1$, this means that anything raised to the zero power is 1. For example: $(28x^2y)^0 = 1$
Example	***Evaluate.*** $\left(\frac{1}{3}\right)^{-2} =$ Use negative exponent's rule: $\left(\frac{1}{x^a}\right)^{-2} = (x^a)^2 \rightarrow \left(\frac{1}{3}\right)^{-2} = (3)^2 =$ Then: $(3)^2 = 9$
Your Turn! **Find more at** bit.ly/3rnkh4	1) $2^{-4} =$ 2) $4^{-3} =$ 3) $7^{-3} =$ 4) $1^{-3} =$ 5) $8^{-3} =$ 6) $4^{-4} =$ 7) $10^{-3} =$ 8) $7^{-4} =$ 9) $\left(\frac{1}{6}\right)^{-1} =$ 10) $\left(\frac{1}{9}\right)^{-2} =$

Topic	Zero and Negative Exponents - Answers
Notes	✓ A negative exponent is the reciprocal of that number with a positive exponent. $(3)^{-2} = \frac{1}{3^2}$ ✓ Zero-Exponent Rule: $a^0 = 1$, this means that anything raised to the zero power is 1. For example: $(28x^2y)^0 = 1$
Example	***Evaluate.*** $\left(\frac{1}{3}\right)^{-2} =$ Use negative exponent's rule: $\left(\frac{1}{x^a}\right)^{-2} = (x^a)^2 \rightarrow \left(\frac{1}{3}\right)^{-2} = (3)^2 =$ Then: $(3)^2 = 9$

Your Turn!		
	1) $2^{-4} = \frac{1}{16}$	2) $4^{-3} = \frac{1}{64}$
	3) $7^{-3} = \frac{1}{343}$	4) $1^{-3} = 1$
	5) $8^{-3} = \frac{1}{512}$	6) $4^{-4} = \frac{1}{256}$
	7) $10^{-3} = \frac{1}{1,000}$	8) $7^{-4} = \frac{1}{2,401}$
	9) $\left(\frac{1}{6}\right)^{-1} = 6$	10) $\left(\frac{1}{9}\right)^{-2} = 81$

Find more at

bit.ly/3rnkh4

Topic	**Negative Exponents and Negative Bases**
Notes	✓ Make the power positive. A negative exponent is the reciprocal of that number with a positive exponent. ✓ The parenthesis is important! 5^{-2} is not the same as $(-5)^{-2}$ $$(-5)^{-2} = -\frac{1}{5^2} \text{ and } (-5)^{-2} = +\frac{1}{5^2}$$
Example	*Simplify.* $\left(-\frac{3x}{4yz}\right)^{-3} =$ Use negative exponent's rule: $\left(\frac{x^a}{x^b}\right)^{-2} = \left(\frac{x^b}{x^a}\right)^2 \rightarrow \left(-\frac{3x}{4yz}\right)^{-3} = \left(-\frac{4yz}{3x}\right)^3$ Now use exponent's rule: $\left(\frac{a}{b}\right)^c = \frac{a^c}{b^c} \rightarrow \left(-\frac{4yz}{3x}\right)^3 = -\frac{4^3 y^3 z^3}{3^3 x^3} = -\frac{64 y^3 z^3}{27 x^3}$

Your Turn!		
	1) $-4x^{-3}y^{-3} =$	2) $25x^{-4}y^{-2} =$
	3) $14a^{-6}b^{-7} =$	4) $-12x^2y^{-3} =$
	5) $-\dfrac{25}{x^{-6}} =$	6) $\dfrac{7b}{-9c^{-4}} =$
Find more at bit.ly/3nPROSM	7) $\dfrac{7ab}{a^{-3}b^{-1}} =$	8) $-\dfrac{5n^{-2}}{10p^{-3}} = -$
	9) $\dfrac{36ab^{-1}}{-3c^{-2}} =$	10) $\left(\dfrac{5a}{3c}\right)^{-2} =$

Topic	Negative Exponents and Negative Bases - Answers
Notes	✓ Make the power positive. A negative exponent is the reciprocal of that number with a positive exponent. ✓ The parenthesis is important! 5^{-2} is not the same as $(-5)^{-2}$ $$(-5)^{-2} = -\frac{1}{5^2} \text{ and } (-5)^{-2} = +\frac{1}{5^2}$$
Example	*Simplify.* $(-\frac{3x}{4yz})^{-3} =$ Use negative exponent's rule: $(\frac{x^a}{x^b})^{-2} = (\frac{x^b}{x^a})^2 \rightarrow (-\frac{3x}{4yz})^{-3} = (-\frac{4yz}{3x})^3$ Now use exponent's rule: $(\frac{a}{b})^c = \frac{a^c}{b^c} \rightarrow (-\frac{4yz}{3x})^3 = -\frac{4^3 y^3 z^3}{3^3 x^3} = -\frac{64 y^3 z^3}{27 x^3}$

Your Turn!		
	1) $-4x^{-3}y^{-3} = -\frac{4}{x^3 y^3}$	2) $25x^{-4}y^{-2} = \frac{25}{x^4 y^2}$
	3) $14a^{-6}b^{-7} = \frac{14}{a^6 b^7}$	4) $-12x^2 y^{-3} = -\frac{12x^2}{y^3}$
	5) $-\frac{25}{x^{-6}} = -25x^6$	6) $\frac{7b}{-9c^{-4}} = -\frac{7bc^4}{9}$
Find more at bit.ly/3nPROSM	7) $\frac{7ab}{a^{-3}b^{-1}} = 7a^4 b^2$	8) $-\frac{5n^{-2}}{10p^{-3}} = -\frac{p^3}{2n^2}$
	9) $\frac{36ab^{-1}}{-3c^{-2}} = -\frac{12ac^2}{b}$	10) $(\frac{5a}{3c})^{-2} = \frac{9c^2}{25a^2}$

Topic	**Scientific Notation**
Notes	✓ It is used to write very big or very small numbers in decimal form. ✓ In scientific notation all numbers are written in the form of: $$m \times 10^n$$ <table><tr><td>**Decimal notation**</td><td>**Scientific notation**</td></tr><tr><td>3</td><td>3×10^0</td></tr><tr><td>$-45,000$</td><td>-4.5×10^4</td></tr><tr><td>0.3</td><td>3×10^{-1}</td></tr><tr><td>2,122.456</td><td>2.122456×10^3</td></tr></table>
Example	*Write 0.00054 in scientific notation.* First, move the decimal point to the right so that you have a number that is between 1 and 10. Then: $m = 5.4$ Now, determine how many places the decimal moved in step 1 by the power of 10. Then: $10^{-4} \rightarrow$ When the decimal moved to the right, the exponent is negative. Then: $0.00054 = 5.4 \times 10^{-4}$
Your Turn! **Find more at** bit.ly/3nOwJYP	1) $0.000452 =$ 2) $0.00016 =$ 3) $52,000,000 =$ 4) $21,000 =$ 5) $3 \times 10^{-1} =$ 6) $5 \times 10^{-2} =$ 7) $1.4 \times 10^4 =$ 8) $3 \times 10^{-5} =$

Topic	Scientific Notation – Answers
Notes	✓ It is used to write very big or very small numbers in decimal form. ✓ In scientific notation all numbers are written in the form of: $$m \times 10^n$$ | Decimal notation	Scientific notation
---	---
3	3×10^0
$-45,000$	-4.5×10^4
0.3	3×10^{-1}
2,122.456	2.122456×10^3	
Example	*Write 0.00054 in scientific notation.* First, move the decimal point to the right so that you have a number that is between 1 and 10. Then: $m = 5.4$ Now, determine how many places the decimal moved in step 1 by the power of 10. Then: $10^{-4} \rightarrow$ When the decimal moved to the right, the exponent is negative. Then: $0.00054 = 5.4 \times 10^{-4}$
Your Turn! **Find more at** bit.ly/3nOwJYP 	1) $0.000452 = 4.52 \times 10^{-4}$ 2) $0.00016 = 1.6 \times 10^{-4}$ 3) $52,000,000 = 5.2 \times 10^7$ 4) $21,000 = 2.1 \times 10^4$ 5) $3 \times 10^{-1} = 0.3$ 6) $5 \times 10^{-2} = 0.05$ 7) $1.4 \times 10^4 = 14,000$ 8) $3 \times 10^{-5} = 0.00003$

Topic	Radicals
Notes	✓ If n is a positive integer and x is a real number, then: $\sqrt[n]{x} = x^{\frac{1}{n}}$, $\sqrt[n]{xy} = x^{\frac{1}{n}} \times y^{\frac{1}{n}}$, $\sqrt[n]{\frac{x}{y}} = \frac{x^{\frac{1}{n}}}{y^{\frac{1}{n}}}$, and $\sqrt[n]{x} \times \sqrt[n]{y} = \sqrt[n]{xy}$ ✓ A square root of x is a number r whose square is: $r^2 = x$ (r is a square root of x. ✓ To add and subtract radicals, we need to have the same values under the radical. For example: $\sqrt{3} + \sqrt{3} = 2\sqrt{3}$, $3\sqrt{5} - \sqrt{5} = 2\sqrt{5}$
Example	*Evaluate.* $\sqrt{32} + \sqrt{8} =$ **Solution:** Since we do not have the same values under the radical, we cannot add these two radicals. But we can simplify each radical. $\sqrt{32} = \sqrt{16} \times \sqrt{2} = 4\sqrt{2}$ and $\sqrt{8} = \sqrt{4} \times \sqrt{2} = 2\sqrt{2}$ Now, we have the same values under the radical. Then: $$\sqrt{32} + \sqrt{8} = 4\sqrt{2} + 2\sqrt{2} = 6\sqrt{2}$$

Your Turn!	1) $\sqrt{6} \times \sqrt{6} =$	2) $\sqrt{12} \times \sqrt{3} =$
	3) $\sqrt{3} \times \sqrt{27} =$	4) $\sqrt{32} \div \sqrt{2} =$
	5) $\sqrt{2} + \sqrt{8} =$	6) $\sqrt{27} - \sqrt{3} =$
Find more at bit.ly/2WEATqr	7) $3\sqrt{7} - 2\sqrt{7} =$	8) $6\sqrt{5} \times 3\sqrt{5} =$

Topic	Radicals - Answers
Notes	✓ If n is a positive integer and x is a real number, then: $\sqrt[n]{x} = x^{\frac{1}{n}}$, $\sqrt[n]{xy} = x^{\frac{1}{n}} \times y^{\frac{1}{n}}$, $\sqrt[n]{\frac{x}{y}} = \frac{x^{\frac{1}{n}}}{y^{\frac{1}{n}}}$, and $\sqrt[n]{x} \times \sqrt[n]{y} = \sqrt[n]{xy}$ ✓ A square root of x is a number r whose square is: $r^2 = x$ (r is a square root of x. ✓ To add and subtract radicals, we need to have the same values under the radical. For example: $\sqrt{3} + \sqrt{3} = 2\sqrt{3}$, $3\sqrt{5} - \sqrt{5} = 2\sqrt{5}$
Example	***Evaluate.*** $\sqrt{32} + \sqrt{8} =$ **Solution:** Since we do not have the same values under the radical, we cannot add these two radicals. But we can simplify each radical. $\sqrt{32} = \sqrt{16} \times \sqrt{2} = 4\sqrt{2}$ and $\sqrt{8} = \sqrt{4} \times \sqrt{2} = 2\sqrt{2}$ Now, we have the same values under the radical. Then: $$\sqrt{32} + \sqrt{8} = 4\sqrt{2} + 2\sqrt{2} = 6\sqrt{2}$$

Your Turn!		
	1) $\sqrt{6} \times \sqrt{6} = 6$	2) $\sqrt{12} \times \sqrt{3} = 6$
	3) $\sqrt{3} \times \sqrt{27} = 9$	4) $\sqrt{32} \div \sqrt{2} = 4$
	5) $\sqrt{2} + \sqrt{8} = 3\sqrt{2}$	6) $\sqrt{27} - \sqrt{3} = 2\sqrt{3}$
Find more at bit.ly/2WEATqr	7) $3\sqrt{7} - 2\sqrt{7} = \sqrt{7}$	8) $6\sqrt{5} \times 3\sqrt{5} = 90$

Topic	Simplifying Polynomials
Notes	✓ Find "like" terms. (they have same variables with same power). ✓ Use "FOIL". (First–Out–In–Last) for binomials: $$(x + a)(x + b) = x^2 + (b + a)x + ab$$ ✓ Add or Subtract "like" terms using order of operation.
Example	***Simplify this expression***. $(x + 3)(x - 8) =$ **Solution:** First apply FOIL method: $(a + b)(c + d) = ac + ad + bc + bd$ $(x + 3)(x - 8) = x^2 - 8x + 3x - 24$ Now combine like terms: $x^2 - 8x + 3x - 24 = x^2 - 5x - 24$

Your Turn!		
	1) $-(4x - 3) =$ _____	2) $3(4x + 7) =$ _____
	3) $3x(3x - 4) =$ _____	4) $5x(2x + 8) =$ _____
	5) $-2x(5x + 6) + 5x =$ _____	6) $-4x(8x - 3) - x^2 =$ _____
Find more at bit.ly/3rnAcj8	7) $(x + 4)(x + 5) =$ _____	8) $(x + 2)(x + 8) =$ _____
	9) $-5x^2 + 9x^3 + 10x^2 =$ _____	10) $-6x^5 + 8x^4 + 9x^5 =$ _____

Topic	Simplifying Polynomials – Answers
Notes	✓ Find "like" terms. (they have same variables with same power). ✓ Use "FOIL". (First–Out–In–Last) for binomials: $$(x + a)(x + b) = x^2 + (b + a)x + ab$$ ✓ Add or Subtract "like" terms using order of operation.
Example	**Simplify this expression.** $(x + 3)(x - 8) =$ **Solution:** First apply FOIL method: $(a + b)(c + d) = ac + ad + bc + bd$ $(x + 3)(x - 8) = x^2 - 8x + 3x - 24$ Now combine like terms: $x^2 - 8x + 3x - 24 = x^2 - 5x - 24$

Your Turn!	1) $-(4x - 3) =$ $-4x + 3$	2) $3(4x + 7) =$ $12x + 21$
	3) $3x(3x - 4) =$ $9x^2 - 12x$	4) $5x(2x + 8) =$ $10x^2 + 40x$
	5) $-2x(5x + 6) + 5x =$ $-10x^2 - 7x$	6) $-4x(8x - 3) - x^2 =$ $-33x^2 + 12x$
	7) $(x + 4)(x + 5) =$ $x^2 + 9x + 20$	8) $(x + 2)(x + 8) =$ $x^2 + 10x + 16$
Find more at bit.ly/3rnAcj8	9) $-5x^2 + 9x^3 + 10x^2 =$ $9x^3 + 5x^2$	10) $-6x^5 + 8x^4 + 9x^5 =$ $3x^5 + 8x^4$

Topic	Adding and Subtracting Polynomials
Notes	✓ Adding polynomials is just a matter of combining like terms, with some order of operations considerations thrown in. ✓ Be careful with the minus signs, and don't confuse addition and multiplication!
Example	*Simplify the expressions*. $(3x^2 - 4x^3) - (5x^3 - 8x^2) =$ **Solution:** First use Distributive Property: $-(5x^3 - 8x^2) = -5x^3 + 8x^2$ $\rightarrow (3x^2 - 4x^3) - (5x^3 - 8x^2) = 3x^2 - 4x^3 - 5x^3 + 8x^2$ Now combine like terms: $3x^2 - 4x^3 - 5x^3 + 8x^2 = -9x^3 + 11x^2$

Your Turn!

1) $(x^2 - 3x) + (2x^2 - 6) =$

_____

2) $(4x^3 + 2x) - (x^3 + 5) =$

_____

3) $(x^2 - 5x) + (6x^2 - 5) =$

_____

4) $(8x^2 - 2) - (3x^2 + 7) =$

_____

5) $(3x^2 + 2) - (2 - 4x^2) =$

_____

6) $(x^3 + x^2) - (x^3 - 10) =$

_____

7) $(3x^3 - 2x) - (x - x^3) =$

_____

8) $(x - 5x^4) - (2x^4 + 3x) =$

_____

Find more at

bit.ly/2KUqHqQ

9) $(8x^3 + 3) - (5 - 4x^3) =$

_____

10) $(9x^2 + 4x^3) - (3x^3 + 2) =$

_____

Topic	**Adding and Subtracting Polynomials – Answers**
Notes	✓ Adding polynomials is just a matter of combining like terms, with some order of operations considerations thrown in. ✓ Be careful with the minus signs, and don't confuse addition and multiplication!
Example	***Simplify the expressions.*** $(3x^2 - 4x^3) - (5x^3 - 8x^2) =$ **Solution:** First use Distributive Property: $-(5x^3 - 8x^2) = -5x^3 + 8x^2$ $\rightarrow (3x^2 - 4x^3) - (5x^3 - 8x^2) = 3x^2 - 4x^3 - 5x^3 + 8x^2$ Now combine like terms: $3x^2 - 4x^3 - 5x^3 + 8x^2 = -9x^3 + 11x^2$

Your Turn!	1) $(x^2 - 3x) + (2x^2 - 6) =$ $3x^2 - 3x - 6$	2) $(4x^3 + 2x) - (x^3 + 5) =$ $3x^3 + 2x - 5$
	3) $(x^2 - 5x) + (6x^2 - 5) =$ $7x^2 - 5x - 5$	4) $(8x^2 - 2) - (3x^2 + 7) =$ $5x^2 - 9$
	5) $(3x^2 + 2) - (2 - 4x^2) =$ $7x^2$	6) $(x^3 + x^2) - (x^3 - 10) =$ $x^2 + 10$
Find more at bit.ly/2KUqHqQ	7) $(3x^3 - 2x) - (x - x^3) =$ $4x^3 - 3x$	8) $(x - 5x^4) - (2x^4 + 3x) =$ $-7x^4 - 2x$
	9) $(8x^3 + 3) - (5 - 4x^3) =$ $12x^3 - 2$	10) $(9x^2 + 4x^3) - (3x^3 + 2) =$ $x^3 + 9x^2 - 2$

Topic	**Multiplying Binomials**
Notes	✓ A binomial is a polynomial that is the sum or the difference of two terms, each of which is a monomial. ✓ To multiply two binomials, use "FOIL" method. (First–Out–In–Last) $(x + a)(x + b) = x \times x + x \times b + a \times x + a \times b = x^2 + bx + ax + ab$
Example	***Multiply.*** $(x - 4)(x + 9) =$ **Solution:** Use "FOIL". (First–Out–In–Last): $(x - 4)(x + 9) = x^2 + 9x - 4x - 36$ Then simplify: $x^2 + 9x - 4x - 36 = x^2 + 5x - 36$
Your Turn! **Find more at** bit.ly/3aCsOFL	1) $(x + 4)(x + 4) =$ _____ 3) $(x - 3)(x + 4) =$ _____ 5) $(x + 3)(x + 4) =$ _____ 7) $(x - 6)(x - 5) =$ _____ 9) $(x + 3)(x - 5) =$ _____ 2) $(x + 4)(x + 3) =$ _____ 4) $(x - 2)(x - 4) =$ _____ 6) $(x + 5)(x + 4) =$ _____ 8) $(x - 5)(x - 5) =$ _____ 10) $(x - 6)(x + 4) =$ _____

Topic	Multiplying Binomials – Answers
Notes	✓A binomial is a polynomial that is the sum or the difference of two terms, each of which is a monomial. ✓To multiply two binomials, use "FOIL" method. (First–Out–In–Last) $(x + a)(x + b) = x \times x + x \times b + a \times x + a \times b = x^2 + bx + ax + ab$
Example	**Multiply.** $(x - 4)(x + 9) =$ **Solution:** Use "FOIL". (First–Out–In–Last): $(x - 4)(x + 9) = x^2 + 9x - 4x - 36$ Then simplify: $x^2 + 9x - 4x - 36 = x^2 + 5x - 36$

Your Turn!	1) $(x + 4)(x + 4) =$ $x^2 + 8x + 16$	2) $(x + 4)(x + 3) =$ $x^2 + 7x + 12$
	3) $(x - 3)(x + 4) =$ $x^2 + x - 12$	4) $(x - 2)(x - 4) =$ $x^2 - 6x + 8$
	5) $(x + 3)(x + 4) =$ $x^2 + 7x + 12$	6) $(x + 5)(x + 4) =$ $x^2 + 9x + 20$
	7) $(x - 6)(x - 5) =$ $x^2 - 11x + 30$	8) $(x - 5)(x - 5) =$ $x^2 - 10x + 25$
Find more at bit.ly/3aCsOFL	9) $(x + 3)(x - 5) =$ $x^2 - 2x - 15$	10) $(x - 6)(x + 4) =$ $x^2 - 2x - 24$

Topic	**Multiplying and Dividing Monomials**
Notes	✓ When you divide or multiply two monomials you need to divide or multiply their coefficients and then divide or multiply their variables. ✓ In case of exponents with the same base, you need to subtract their powers. ✓ Exponent's rules: $$x^a \times x^b = x^{a+b}, \qquad \frac{x^a}{x^b} = x^{a-b}$$ $$\frac{1}{x^b} = x^{-b}, \quad (x^a)^b = x^{a \times b}$$ $$(xy)^a = x^a \times y^a$$
Example	*Divide expressions.* $\dfrac{-18x^5y^6}{2xy^2} =$ **Solution:** Use exponents' division rule: $\dfrac{x^a}{x^b} = x^{a-b}$, $\dfrac{x^5}{x} = x^{5-1} = x^4$ and $\dfrac{y^6}{y^2} = y^4$ Then: $\dfrac{-18x^5y^6}{2xy^2} = -9x^4y^4$
Your Turn!	1) $(x^6y)(xy^3) =$ ____ 　　 2) $(x^5y^2)(x^3y^3) =$ ____
	3) $(x^7y^4)(2x^5y^2) =$ ____ 　　 4) $(3x^5y^4)(4x^6y^3) =$ ____
	5) $(-6x^8y^7)(4x^6y^9) =$ ____ 　　 6) $(-2x^9y^3)(9x^7y^8) =$ ____
Find more at bit.ly/2WHp4Q4	7) $\dfrac{40x^9y^6}{8x^5y^4} =$ ____ 　　 8) $\dfrac{-56x^{10}y^{15}}{8x^8y^9} =$ ____

Topic	Multiplying and Dividing Monomials - Answers
Notes	✓ When you divide or multiply two monomials you need to divide or multiply their coefficients and then divide or multiply their variables. ✓ In case of exponents with the same base, you need to subtract their powers. ✓ Exponent's rules: $$x^a \times x^b = x^{a+b}, \qquad \frac{x^a}{x^b} = x^{a-b}$$ $$\frac{1}{x^b} = x^{-b}, \quad (x^a)^b = x^{a \times b}$$ $$(xy)^a = x^a \times y^a$$
Example	**Divide expressions.** $\frac{-18x^5y^6}{2xy^2} =$ **Solution:** Use exponents' division rule: $\frac{x^a}{x^b} = x^{a-b}, \frac{x^5}{x} = x^{5-1} = x^4$ and $\frac{y^6}{y^2} = y^4$ Then: $\frac{-18x^5y^6}{2xy^2} = -9x^4y^4$
Your Turn!	1) $(x^6y)(xy^3) =$ x^7y^4 2) $(x^5y^2)(x^3y^3) =$ x^8y^5
	3) $(x^7y^4)(2x^5y^2) =$ $2x^{12}y^6$ 4) $(3x^5y^4)(4x^6y^3) =$ $12x^{11}y^7$
	5) $(-6x^8y^7)(4x^6y^9) =$ $-24x^{14}y^{16}$ 6) $(-2x^9y^3)(9x^7y^8) =$ $-18x^{16}y^{11}$
Find more at bit.ly/2WHp4Q4	7) $\frac{40x^9y^6}{8x^5y^4} =$ $5x^4y^2$ 8) $\frac{-56x^{10}y^{15}}{8x^8y^9} =$ $-7x^2y^6$

Topic	Multiplying a Polynomial and a Monomial
Notes	✓ When multiplying monomials, use the product rule for exponents. $x^a \times x^b = x^{a+b}$ ✓ When multiplying a monomial by a polynomial, use the distributive property. $$a \times (b + c) = a \times b + a \times c = ab + ac$$ $$a \times (b - c) = a \times b - a \times c = ab - ac$$
Example	***Multiply expressions.*** $4x(5x - 8) =$ **Solution:** Use Distributive Property: $4x(5x - 8) = 4x \times 5x - 4x \times (8) =$ Now, simplify: $4x \times 5x - 4x \times (8) = 20x^2 - 32x$
Your Turn!	1) $4x(3x + y) =$ ⎯⎯⎯⎯ 2) $x(x - 6y) =$ ⎯⎯⎯⎯
	3) $-x(5x - 3y) =$ ⎯⎯⎯⎯ 4) $4x(x + 5y) =$ ⎯⎯⎯⎯
	5) $-x(5x + 8y) =$ ⎯⎯⎯⎯ 6) $2x(6x - 7y) =$ ⎯⎯⎯⎯
Find more at bit.ly/3aBYdx2	7) $-4x(x^3 + 3y^2 - 7x) =$ ⎯⎯⎯⎯ 8) $6x(x^2 - 4y^2 + 3) =$ ⎯⎯⎯⎯

Topic	Multiplying a Polynomial and a Monomial - Answers
Notes	✓ When multiplying monomials, use the product rule for exponents. $x^a \times x^b = x^{a+b}$ ✓ When multiplying a monomial by a polynomial, use the distributive property. $$a \times (b + c) = a \times b + a \times c = ab + ac$$ $$a \times (b - c) = a \times b - a \times c = ab - ac$$
Example	*Multiply expressions.* $4x(5x - 8) =$ **Solution:** Use Distributive Property: $4x(5x - 8) = 4x \times 5x - 4x \times (8) =$ Now, simplify: $4x \times 5x - 4x \times (8) = 20x^2 - 32x$

Your Turn!
 	
Find more at
 	
bit.ly/3aBYdx2
	1) $4x(3x + y) =$
	    $12x^2 + 4xy$ 2) $x(x - 6y) =$
	    $x^2 - 6xy$
	
	3) $-x(5x - 3y) =$
	    $-5x^2 + 3xy$ 4) $4x(x + 5y) =$
	    $4x^2 + 20xy$
	
	5) $-x(5x + 8y) =$
	    $-5x^2 - 8xy$ 6) $2x(6x - 7y) =$
	    $12x^2 - 14xy$
	
	7) $-4x(x^3 + 3y^2 - 7x) =$
	    $-4x^4 - 12xy^2 + 28x^2$ 8) $6x(x^2 - 4y^2 + 3) =$
	    $6x^3 - 24xy^2 + 18x$

Topic	Multiplying Monomials
Notes	✓ A monomial is a polynomial with just one term: Examples: $5x$ or $7x^2yz^8$. ✓ When you multiply monomials, first multiply the coefficients (a number placed before and multiplying the variable) and then multiply the variables using multiplication property of exponents. $x^a \times x^b = x^{a+b}$
Example	***Multiply.*** $(-3xy^4z^5) \times (2x^2y^5z^2) =$ **Solution:** Multiply coefficients and find same variables and use multiplication property of exponents: $x^a \times x^b = x^{a+b}$ $-3 \times 2 = -6, x \times x^2 = x^{1+2} = x^3$, $y^4 \times y^5 = y^{4+5} = y^9$, and $z^2 \times z^5 = z^{2+5} = z^7$ Then: $(-3xy^4z^5) \times (2x^2y^5z^2) = -6x^3y^9z^7$
Your Turn! **Find more at** bit.ly/2KLVoP8 	1) $3x^2 \times 5x^6 =$ _____ 2) $6x^7 \times 2x^4 =$ _____ 3) $-2x^2y^4 \times 6x^3y^2 =$ _____ 4) $-5x^5y \times 3x^3y^4 =$ _____ 5) $8x^7y^5 \times 5x^6y^3 =$ _____ 6) $-6x^7y^5 \times (-3x^9y^8) =$ _____ 7) $14x^8y^8z^4 \times 2x^4y^3z =$ _____ 8) $-7x^9y^7z^{11} \times 6x^6y^7z^5 =$ _____

Topic	**Multiplying Monomials**- Answers
Notes	✓ A monomial is a polynomial with just one term: Examples: $5x$ or $7x^2yz^8$. ✓ When you multiply monomials, first multiply the coefficients (a number placed before and multiplying the variable) and then multiply the variables using multiplication property of exponents. $x^a \times x^b = x^{a+b}$
Example	***Multiply.*** $(-3xy^4z^5) \times (2x^2y^5z^2) =$ **Solution:** Multiply coefficients and find same variables and use multiplication property of exponents: $x^a \times x^b = x^{a+b}$ $-3 \times 2 = -6$, $x \times x^2 = x^{1+2} = x^3$, $y^4 \times y^5 = y^{4+5} = y^9$, and $z^2 \times z^5 = z^{2+5} = z^7$ Then: $(-3xy^4z^5) \times (2x^2y^5z^2) = -6x^3y^9z^7$

Your Turn!	1) $3x^2 \times 5x^6 =$
	    $15x^8$
		2) $6x^7 \times 2x^4 =$
		    $12x^{11}$

	3) $-2x^2y^4 \times 6x^3y^2 =$
	    $-12x^5y^6$
		4) $-5x^5y \times 3x^3y^4 =$
		    $-15x^8y^5$

	5) $8x^7y^5 \times 5x^6y^3 =$
	    $40x^{13}y^8$
		6) $-6x^7y^5 \times (-3x^9y^8) =$
		    $18x^{16}y^{13}$

Find more at bit.ly/2KLVoP8 	7) $14x^8y^8z^4 \times 2x^4y^3z =$ $28x^{12}y^{11}z^5$	8) $-7x^9y^7z^{11} \times 6x^6y^7z^5 =$ $-42x^{15}y^{14}z^{16}$

Topic	Factoring Trinomials
Notes	To factor trinomial, use of the following methods: ✓ "FOIL": $(x + a)(x + b) = x^2 + (b + a)x + ab$ ✓ "Difference of Squares": $$a^2 - b^2 = (a + b)(a - b)$$ $$a^2 + 2ab + b^2 = (a + b)(a + b)$$ $$a^2 - 2ab + b^2 = (a - b)(a - b)$$ ✓ "Reverse FOIL": $x^2 + (b + a)x + ab = (x + a)(x + b)$
Example	***Factor this trinomial.*** $x^2 + 12x + 32 =$ **Solution:** Break the expression into groups: $(x^2 + 4x) + (8x + 32)$ Now factor out x from $x^2 + 4x$: $x(x + 4)$, and factor out 8 from $8x + 32$: $8(x + 4)$ Then: $(x^2 + 4x) + (8x + 32) = x(x + 4) + 8(x + 4)$ Now factor out like term: $(x + 4) \rightarrow (x + 4)(x + 8)$
Your Turn!	1) $x^2 + 3x - 4 =$ _____ 2) $x^2 + 4x - 12 =$ _____
	3) $x^2 + x - 12 =$ _____ 4) $x^2 - 6x + 8 =$ _____
Find more at bit.ly/38EpdJA	5) $x^2 + 7x + 12 =$ _____ 6) $x^2 + 12x + 32 =$ _____
	7) $x^2 + 13x + 30 =$ _____ 8) $x^2 - x + 72 =$ _____

Topic	Factoring Trinomials – Answers
Notes	To factor trinomial, use of the following methods: ✓ "FOIL": $(x + a)(x + b) = x^2 + (b + a)x + ab$ ✓ "Difference of Squares": $$a^2 - b^2 = (a + b)(a - b)$$ $$a^2 + 2ab + b^2 = (a + b)(a + b)$$ $$a^2 - 2ab + b^2 = (a - b)(a - b)$$ ✓ "Reverse FOIL": $x^2 + (b + a)x + ab = (x + a)(x + b)$
Example	**Factor this trinomial.** $x^2 + 12x + 32 =$ **Solution:** Break the expression into groups: $(x^2 + 4x) + (8x + 32)$ Now factor out x from $x^2 + 4x : x(x + 4)$, and factor out 8 from $8x + 32$: $8(x + 4)$ Then: $(x^2 + 4x) + (8x + 32) = x(x + 4) + 8(x + 4)$ Now factor out like term: $(x + 4) \rightarrow (x + 4)(x + 8)$

Your Turn!	1) $x^2 + 3x - 4 =$ $(x + 4)(x - 1)$	2) $x^2 + 4x - 12 =$ $(x - 2)(x + 6)$
	3) $x^2 + x - 12 =$ $(x - 3)(x + 4)$	4) $x^2 - 6x + 8 =$ $(x - 2)(x - 4)$
Find more at bit.ly/38EpdJA	5) $x^2 + 7x + 12 =$ $(x + 3)(x + 4)$	6) $x^2 + 12x + 32 =$ $(x + 8)(x + 4)$
	7) $x^2 + 13x + 30 =$ $(x + 10)(x + 3)$	8) $x^2 - x - 72 =$ $(x - 9)(x + 8)$

Topic	**The Pythagorean Theorem**
Notes	✓ In any right triangle: $a^2 + b^2 = c^2$
Example	Right triangle ABC (not shown) has two legs of lengths 18 cm (AB) and 24 cm (AC). What is the length of the third side (BC)? **Solution:** Use Pythagorean Theorem: $a^2 + b^2 = c^2$ Then: $a^2 + b^2 = c^2 \rightarrow 18^2 + 24^2 = c^2 \rightarrow 324 + 576 = c^2$ $c^2 = 900 \rightarrow c = \sqrt{900} = 30\ cm$
Your Turn!	

Your Turn!

1) _____

8, ?, 6

2) _____

34, 16, ?

3) _____

13, 5, ?

4) _____

10, ?, 8

Find more at

bit.ly/37Jl08v

Topic	The Pythagorean Theorem – Answers
Notes	✓ In any right triangle: $a^2 + b^2 = c^2$
Example	Right triangle ABC (not shown) has two legs of lengths 18 cm (AB) and 24 cm (AC). What is the length of the third side (BC)? **Solution:** Use Pythagorean Theorem: $a^2 + b^2 = c^2$ Then: $a^2 + b^2 = c^2 \rightarrow 18^2 + 24^2 = c^2 \rightarrow 324 + 576 = c^2$ $c^2 = 900 \rightarrow c = \sqrt{900} = 30 \, cm$

Your Turn!

1) 10

2) 30

3) 12

4) 6

Find more at

bit.ly/37Jl08v

Topic	**Triangles**
Notes	✓ In any triangle the sum of all angles is 180 degrees. ✓ 0Area of a triangle = $\frac{1}{2}(base \times height)$ h b
Example	*What is the area of the following triangle?* 6 16 **Solution:** Use the area formula: Area $= \frac{1}{2}(base \times height)$ $base = 16$ and $height = 6$ Area $= \frac{1}{2}(16 \times 6) = \frac{96}{2} = 48$
Your Turn! **Find more at** bit.ly/3haZrRg	1) _____ 20 12 2) _____ 18 28 3) _____ 20 30 4) _____ 34 40

Topic	Triangles – Answers
Notes	✓ In any triangle the sum of all angles is 180 degrees. ✓ Area of a triangle = $\frac{1}{2} (base \times height)$
Example	**What is the area of the following triangle?** **Solution:** Use the area formula: Area = $\frac{1}{2} (base \times height)$ $base = 16$ and $height = 6$ Area = $\frac{1}{2}(16 \times 6) = \frac{96}{2} = 48$

Your Turn!	1) 120	2) 252
	3) 300	4) 680

Find more at

bit.ly/3haZrRg

Topic	Polygons
Notes	Perimeter of a square $= 4 \times side = 4s$ Perimeter of a rectangle $= 2(width + length)$ Perimeter of trapezoid $= a + b + c + d$ Perimeter of a regular hexagon $= 6a$ Perimeter of a parallelogram $= 2(l + w)$
Example	**Find the perimeter of following regular hexagon.** **Solution:** Since the hexagon is regular, all sides are equal. Then: Perimeter of Hexagon $= 6 \times (one\ side)$ Perimeter of Hexagon $= 6 \times (one\ side) = 6 \times 9 = 54\ m$

Your Turn!	5) *(rectangle)* _____	6) _____
	8 *in* 12 *in*	8 m 10 m 10 m 14 m

7) *(regular hexagon)* _____ 5 m	8) *(parallelogram)* _____ 9 in 11 in

Topic	Polygons – Answers
Notes	Perimeter of a square $= 4 \times side = 4s$ Perimeter of a rectangle $= 2(width + length)$ Perimeter of trapezoid $= a + b + c + d$ Perimeter of a regular hexagon $= 6a$ Perimeter of a parallelogram $= 2(l + w)$
Example	*Find the perimeter of following regular hexagon.* **Solution:** Since the hexagon is regular, all sides are equal. Then: Perimeter of Hexagon $= 6 \times (one\ side)$ Perimeter of Hexagon $= 6 \times (one\ side) = 6 \times 9 = 54\ m$

Your Turn!	5) *(rectangle)* 40 in 8 in 12 in	6) 42 m 8 m 10 m 10 m 14 m
Find more at bit.ly/3nFNiGi	7) *(regular hexagon)* 30 m 5 m	8) *(parallelogram)* 40 in 9 in 11 in

Topic	Circles
Notes	✓ In a circle, variable r is usually used for the radius and d for diameter and π is about 3.14. ✓ $Area\ of\ a\ circle = \pi r^2$ ✓ $Circumference\ of\ a\ circle = 2\pi r$ *(circle diagram with radius r)*
Example	**Find the area of the circle.** Solution: Use area formula: $Area = \pi r^2$ $r = 2\ in \rightarrow Area = \pi(2)^2 = 4\pi,\ \pi = 3.14$ **Then:** $Area = 4 \times 3.14 = 12.56\ in^2$ *(circle diagram with 2 in)*
Your Turn!	**Find the area of each circle.** ($\pi = 3.14$) 1) _____ *(circle, 5 cm)* 2) _____ *(circle, 10 in)* **Find the Circumference of each circle.** ($\pi = 3.14$) 3) _____ *(circle, 8 cm)* 4) _____ *(circle, 7 m)*

Find more at

bit.ly/3nJdOP2

Topic	Circles – Answers
Notes	✓ In a circle, variable r is usually used for the radius and d for diameter and π is about 3.14. ✓ $Area\ of\ a\ circle = \pi r^2$ ✓ $Circumference\ of\ a\ circle = 2\pi r$
Example	***Find the area of the circle.*** Solution: Use area formula: $Area = \pi r^2$ $r = 2\ in \rightarrow Area = \pi(2)^2 = 4\pi, \pi = 3.14$ ***Then:*** $Area = 4 \times 3.14 = 12.56\ in^2$

Your Turn!

Find the area of each circle. ($\pi = 3.14$)

1) $78.5cm^2$

2) $314\ in^2$

Find the Circumference of each circle. ($\pi = 3.14$)

3) $50.24\ cm$

4) $43.96\ m$

Find more at

bit.ly/3nJdOP2

Topic	Cubes
Notes	✓ A cube is a three-dimensional solid object bounded by six square sides. ✓ Volume is the measure of the amount of space inside of a solid figure, like a cube, ball, cylinder or pyramid. ✓ Volume of a cube $= (one\ side)^3$ ✓ surface area of cube $= 6 \times (one\ side)^2$
Example	**Find the volume and surface area of the following cube.** $15\ cm$ **Solution:** Use volume formula: $volume = (one\ side)^3$ Then: $volume = (one\ side)^3 = (15)^3 = 3{,}375\ cm^3$ Use surface area formula: $surface\ area\ of\ cube: 6(one\ side)^2 = 6(15)^2 = 6(225) = 1{,}350\ cm^2$
Your Turn!	**Find the volume of each cube.**

1) _____

$9\ in$

2) _____

$13\ ft$

3) _____

$14\ cm$

4) _____

$20\ m$

Find more at

bit.ly/2M6PfOl

Topic	Cubes – Answers
Notes	✓ A cube is a three-dimensional solid object bounded by six square sides. ✓ Volume is the measure of the amount of space inside of a solid figure, like a cube, ball, cylinder or pyramid. ✓ Volume of a cube $= (one\ side)^3$ ✓ surface area of cube $= 6 \times (one\ side)^2$
Example	***Find the volume and surface area of the following cube.*** 15 cm **Solution:** Use volume formula: $volume = (one\ side)^3$ Then: $volume = (one\ side)^3 = (15)^3 = 3,375\ cm^3$ Use surface area formula: $surface\ area\ of\ cube: 6(one\ side)^2 = 6(15)^2 = 6(225) = 1,350\ cm^2$
Your Turn!	***Find the volume of each cube.***

1) $729\ in^3$

9 in

2) $2,197\ ft^3$

13 ft

3) $2,744\ cm^3$

14 cm

4) $8,000\ m^3$

20 m

Topic	Trapezoids
Notes	✓ A quadrilateral with at least one pair of parallel sides is a trapezoid. ✓ Area of a trapezoid $= \frac{1}{2}h(b_1 + b_2)$

Example	**Calculate the area of the trapezoid.**
	   Solution:
	   Use area formula: $A = \frac{1}{2}h(b_1 + b_2)$
	   $b_1 = 8\ cm$, $b_2 = 12\ cm$ and $h = 14\ cm$
	   Then: $A = \frac{1}{2}(14)(12 + 8) = 7(20) = 140\ cm^2$

Your Turn!
 	
Find more at
bit.ly/3hpKACJ
	1) _____
	   7 cm, 4 cm, 10 cm
	
	2) _____
	   8 m, 10 m, 12 m
	
	3) _____
	   7 ft, 6 ft, 15 ft
	
	4) _____
	   8 cm, 6 cm, 12 cm

Topic	Trapezoids – Answers
Notes	✓ A quadrilateral with at least one pair of parallel sides is a trapezoid. ✓ Area of a trapezoid $= \frac{1}{2}h(b_1 + b_2)$
Example	**Calculate the area of the trapezoid.** Solution: Use area formula: $A = \frac{1}{2}h(b_1 + b_2)$ $b_1 = 8\ cm$, $b_2 = 12\ cm$ and $h = 14\ cm$ Then: $A = \frac{1}{2}(14)(12 + 8) = 7(20) = 140\ cm^2$

Your Turn!

1) $34\ cm^2$

7 cm

4 cm

10 cm

2) $100\ m^2$

8 m

10 m

12 m

3) $66\ ft^2$

7 ft

6 ft

15 ft

4) $60\ cm^2$

8 cm

6 cm

12 cm

Find more at

bit.ly/3hpKACJ

Topic	**Rectangular Prisms**
Notes	✓ A solid 3-dimensional object which has six rectangular faces. ✓ Volume of a Rectangular prism = $\boldsymbol{Length \times Width \times Height}$ $Volume = l \times w \times h$ $Surface\ area = 2(wh + lw + lh)$
Example	***Find the volume and surface area of rectangular prism.*** **Solution:** Use volume formula: $Volume = l \times w \times h$ Then: $Volume = 4 \times 2 \times 6 = 48\ m^3$ Use surface area formula: $Surface\ area = 2(wh + lw + lh)$ Then: $Surface\ area = 2\big((2 \times 6) + (4 \times 2) + (4 \times 6)\big)$ $\qquad\qquad = 2(12 + 8 + 24) = 2(44) = 88\ m^2$
Your Turn!	***Find the surface area of each Rectangular Prism.***

1) _____

5 ft   10 ft   3 ft

2) _____

8 cm   16 cm   6 cm

3) _____

12 m   18 m   10 m

4) _____

18 in   16 in   12 in

Find more at

bit.ly/3nKm2GT

Topic	Rectangular Prisms - Answers
Notes	✓ A solid 3-dimensional object which has six rectangular faces. ✓ Volume of a Rectangular prism = **Length × Width × Height** $Volume = l \times w \times h$ $Surface\ area = 2(wh + lw + lh)$

Example

Find the volume and surface area of rectangular prism.
Solution:
Use volume formula: $Volume = l \times w \times h$

Then: $Volume = 4 \times 2 \times 6 = 48\ m^3$

Use surface area formula: $Surface\ area = 2(wh + lw + lh)$

Then: $Surface\ area = 2\big((2 \times 6) + (4 \times 2) + (4 \times 6)\big)$

$\qquad\qquad = 2(12 + 8 + 24) = 2(44) = 88\ m^2$

4 m, 6 m, 2 m

Your Turn!   *Find the surface area of each Rectangular Prism.*

1) $190\ ft^2$

5 ft, 10 ft, 3 ft

2) $544\ cm^2$

8 cm, 16 cm, 6 cm

3) $1,032\ m^2$

12 m, 18 m, 10 m

4) $1,392\ in^2$

18 in, 16 in, 12 in

Find more at

bit.ly/3nKm2GT

Topic	Cylinder
Notes	✓ A cylinder is a solid geometric figure with straight parallel sides and a circular or oval cross section. ✓ *Volume of Cylinder Formula* $= \pi(radius)^2 \times height$ $\pi = 3.14$ ✓ *Surface area of a cylinder* $= 2\pi r^2 + 2\pi r h$ *height* *radius*
Example	**Find the volume and Surface area of the follow Cylinder.** **Solution:** Use volume formula: $Volume = \pi(radius)^2 \times height$ Then: $Volume = \pi(3)^2 \times 12 = 9\pi \times 12 = 108\pi$ $\pi = 3.14$ **then:** $Volume = 108\pi = 339.12 \ cm^3$ Use surface area formula: $Surface\ area = 2\pi r^2 + 2\pi r h$ **Then:** $2\pi(3)^2 + 2\pi(3)(12) = 2\pi(9) + 2\pi(36) = 18\pi + 72\pi = 90\pi$ $\pi = 3.14$ **Then:** $Surface\ area = 90 \times 3.14 = 282.6 \ cm^2$ $12\ cm$ $3\ cm$
Your Turn! **Find more at** bit.ly/37LtcVM	**Find the volume of each Cylinder.** ($\pi = 3.14$) 1) _____ $8\ in$ $3\ in$ 2) _____ $14\ m$ $5\ m$ **Find the Surface area of each Cylinder.** ($\pi = 3.14$) 3) _____ $15\ ft$ $9\ ft$ 4) _____ $12\ cm$ $6\ cm$

Topic	Cylinder – Answers
Notes	✓ A cylinder is a solid geometric figure with straight parallel sides and a circular or oval cross section. ✓ *Volume of Cylinder Formula = π(radius)² × height π = 3.14* ✓ *Surface area of a cylinder = 2πr² + 2πrh* height radius
Example	**Find the volume and Surface area of the follow Cylinder.** Solution: Use volume formula: $Volume = \pi(radius)^2 \times height$ Then: $Volume = \pi(3)^2 \times 12 = 9\pi \times 12 = 108\pi$ $\pi = 3.14$ *then:* $Volume = 108\pi = 339.12\ cm^3$ Use surface area formula: $Surface\ area = 2\pi r^2 + 2\pi rh$ **Then:** $2\pi(3)^2 + 2\pi(3)(12) = 2\pi(9) + 2\pi(36) = 18\pi + 72\pi = 90\pi$ $\pi = 3.14$ **Then:** $Surface\ area = 90 \times 3.14 = 282.6\ cm^2$ 12 cm 3 cm
Your Turn!	**Find the volume of each Cylinder.** (π = 3.14)

1) $226.08\ in^3$ 8 in 3 in	2) $1,099\ m^3$ 14 m 5 m

Find the Surface area of each Cylinder. (π = 3.14)

3) $1,356.48\ ft^2$ 15 ft 9 ft	4) $678.24\ cm^2$ 12 cm 6 cm

Find more at

bit.ly/37LtcVM

Topic	Mean, Median, Mode, and Range of the Given Data
Notes	✓ Mean: $\dfrac{sum\ of\ the\ data}{total\ number\ of\ data\ entires}$ ✓ Mode: value in the list that appears most often. ✓ Median: is the middle number of a group of numbers that have been arranged in order by size. ✓ Range: the difference of largest value and smallest value in the list.
Example	***Find the mode and median of these numbers?*** $16, 10, 6, 3, 1, 16, 2, 4$ **Solution:** Mode: value in the list that appears most often. Number 16 is the value in the list that appears most often (there are two number 16). To find median, write the numbers in order: $1, 2, 3, 4, 6, 10, 16, 16$ Number 4 and 6 are in the middle. Find their average: $\dfrac{4+6}{2} = \dfrac{10}{2} = 5$ The median is 5.

Your Turn!	1) $5, 2, 4, 8, 5, 6$ Mode: _____ Range: _____ Mean: _____ Median: _____	2) $6, 3, 2, 9, 5, 7, 2, 14$ Mode: _____ Range: _____ Mean: _____ Median: _____
Find more at bit.ly/2KO86gg	3) $5, 4, 3, 2, 9, 5, 6, 8, 12$ Mode: _____ Range: _____ Mean: _____ Median: _____	4) $10, 3, 8, 3, 9, 3, 4, 14$ Mode: _____ Range: _____ Mean: _____ Median: _____

Topic	Mean, Median, Mode, and Range of the Given Data - Answers
Notes	✓ Mean: $\dfrac{sum\ of\ the\ data}{total\ number\ of\ data\ entires}$ ✓ Mode: value in the list that appears most often. ✓ Median: is the middle number of a group of numbers that have been arranged in order by size. ✓ Range: the difference of largest value and smallest value in the list.
Example	***Find the mode and median of these numbers?*** $16, 10, 6, 3, 1, 16, 2, 4$ **Solution:** Mode: value in the list that appears most often. Number 16 is the value in the list that appears most often (there are two number 16). To find median, write the numbers in order: $1, 2, 3, 4, 6, 10, 16, 16$ Number 4 and 6 are in the middle. Find their average: $\dfrac{4+6}{2} = \dfrac{10}{2} = 5$ The median is 5.

Your Turn!		
	1) $5, 2, 4, 8, 5, 6$ Mode: 5 Range: 6 Mean: 5 Median: 5	2) $6, 3, 2, 9, 5, 7, 2, 14$ Mode: 2 Range: 12 Mean: 6 Median: 5.5
Find more at bit.ly/2KO86gg 	3) $5, 4, 3, 2, 9, 5, 6, 8, 12$ Mode: 5 Range: 10 Mean: 6 Median: 5	4) $10, 3, 8, 3, 9, 3, 4, 14$ Mode: 3 Range: 11 Mean: 6.75 Median: 6

Topic	Probability Problems
Notes	✓ Probability is the likelihood of something happening in the future. It is expressed as a number between zero (can never happen) to 1 (will always happen). ✓ Probability can be expressed as a fraction, a decimal, or a percent. ✓ Probability formula: $Probability = \frac{number\ of\ desired\ outcomes}{number\ of\ total\ outcomes}$
Example	*If there are 3 green balls, 4 red balls, and 10 blue balls in a basket, what is the probability that Jason will pick out a red ball from the basket?* **Solution:** There are 4 red ball and 17 are total number of balls. Therefore, probability that Jason will pick out a red ball from the basket is 4 out of 17 or $\frac{4}{3+4+10} = \frac{4}{17}$
Your Turn!	1) A number is chosen at random from 1 to 15. Find the probability of selecting a prime number. (A prime number is a whole number that is only divisible by itself and 1) _____
	2) There are only red and blue cards in a box. The probability of choosing a red card in the box at random is one third. If there are 24 blue cards, how many cards are in the box? _____
Find more at bit.ly/3phwk1p	3) A die is rolled, what is the probability that an odd number is obtained? _____

Topic	Probability Problems – Answers
Notes	✓ Probability is the likelihood of something happening in the future. It is expressed as a number between zero (can never happen) to 1 (will always happen). ✓ Probability can be expressed as a fraction, a decimal, or a percent. ✓ Probability formula: $Probability = \frac{number\ of\ desired\ outcomes}{number\ of\ total\ outcomes}$
Example	***If there are 3 green balls, 4 red balls, and 10 blue balls in a basket, what is the probability that Jason will pick out a red ball from the basket?*** **Solution:** There are 4 red ball and 17 are total number of balls. Therefore, probability that Jason will pick out a red ball from the basket is 4 out of 17 or $\frac{4}{3+4+10} = \frac{4}{17}$
Your Turn! **Find more at** bit.ly/3phwk1p 	1) A number is chosen at random from 1 to 15. Find the probability of selecting a prime number. (A prime number is a whole number that is only divisible by itself and 1) $\frac{6}{15} = \frac{2}{5}$ *(There are 6 prime numbers from 1 to 15: 2, 3, 5, 7, 11, 13)*
	2) There are only red and blue cards in a box. The probability of choosing a red card in the box at random is one third. If there are 24 blue cards, how many cards are in the box? 36
	3) A die is rolled, what is the probability that an odd number is obtained? $\frac{1}{2}$

Topic	Pie Graph
Notes	✓ A Pie Chart is a circle chart divided into sectors, each sector represents the relative size of each value.
Example	A library has 460 books that include Mathematics, Physics, Chemistry, English and History. Use following graph to answer the question. **What is the number of Physics books?** **Solution:** Number of total books $= 460$ Percent of Physics books $= 25\% = 0.25$ Then, umber of Physics books: $$0.25 \times 460 = 115$$
Your Turn! **Find more at** bit.ly/34ECTDv 	The circle graph below shows all Mr. Smith's expenses for last month. Mr. Smith spent \$400 for clothes last month. Mr. Smith's last month expenses
	1) How much did Mr. Smith spend for his Books last month? _____ 2) How much did Mr. Smith spend for Bills last month? _____ 3) How much did Mr. Smith spend for his foods last month? _____

Topic	Pie Graph
Notes	✓ A Pie Chart is a circle chart divided into sectors, each sector represents the relative size of each value.
Example	A library has 460 books that include Mathematics, Physics, Chemistry, English and History. Use following graph to answer the question. **What is the number of Physics books?** **Solution:** Number of total books = 460 Percent of Physics books = 25% = 0.25 Then, umber of Physics books: $$0.25 \times 460 = 115$$ History 10% Mathematics 30% English 15% Chemistry 20% Physics 25%
Your Turn!	The circle graph below shows all Mr. Smith's expenses for last month. Mr. Smith spent $400 for clothes last month. Bills 20% Foods 25% Others 23% Clothes 20% Books 12% Mr. Smith's last month expenses
Find more at bit.ly/34ECTDv	1) How much did Mr. Smith spend for his Books last month? $240 2) How much did Mr. Smith spend for Bills last month? $400 3) How much did Mr. Smith spend for his foods last month? $500

Topic	**Permutations and Combinations**
Notes	✓ Permutations: The number of ways to choose a sample of k elements from a set of n distinct objects where order does matter, and replacements are not allowed. For a permutation problem, use this formula: $$_nP_k = \frac{n!}{(n-k)!}$$ ✓ Combination: The number of ways to choose a sample of r elements from a set of n distinct objects where order does not matter, and replacements are not allowed. For a combination problem, use this formula: $$_nC_r = \frac{n!}{r!\,(n-r)!}$$ ✓ Factorials are products, indicated by an exclamation mark. For example, 4! Equals: $4 \times 3 \times 2 \times 1$. Remember that 0! is defined to be equal to 1.
Example	***How many ways can we pick a team of 4 people from a group of 8?*** **Solution:** Since the order doesn't matter, we need to use combination formula where n is 8 and r is 4. Then: $\frac{n!}{r!\,(n-r)!} = \frac{8!}{4!\,(8-4)!} = \frac{8!}{4!\,(4)!} = \frac{8\times7\times6\times5\times4!}{4!\,(4)!} = \frac{8\times7\times6\times5}{4\times3\times2\times1} = \frac{1,680}{24} = 70$
Your Turn! **Find more at** bit.ly/34BQgUY	1) In how many ways can 6 athletes be arranged in a straight line? _____
	2) How many ways can we award a first and second place prize among eight contestants? _____
	3) In how many ways can we choose 4 players from a team of 10 players? _____

Topic	Permutations and Combinations – Answers
Notes	✓ Permutations: The number of ways to choose a sample of k elements from a set of n distinct objects where order does matter, and replacements are not allowed. For a permutation problem, use this formula: $$_nP_k = \frac{n!}{(n-k)!}$$ ✓ Combination: The number of ways to choose a sample of r elements from a set of n distinct objects where order does not matter, and replacements are not allowed. For a combination problem, use this formula: $$_nC_r = \frac{n!}{r!\,(n-r)!}$$ ✓ Factorials are products, indicated by an exclamation mark. For example, 4! Equals: $4 \times 3 \times 2 \times 1$. Remember that 0! is defined to be equal to 1.
Example	***How many ways can we pick a team of 4 people from a group of 8?*** **Solution:** Since the order doesn't matter, we need to use combination formula where n is 8 and r is 4. Then: $\frac{n!}{r!\,(n-r)!} = \frac{8!}{4!\,(8-4)!} = \frac{8!}{4!\,(4)!} = \frac{8\times7\times6\times5\times4!}{4!\,(4)!} = \frac{8\times7\times6\times5}{4\times3\times2\times1} = \frac{1,680}{24} = 70$
Your Turn! **Find more at** bit.ly/34BQgUY	1) In how many ways can 6 athletes be arranged in a straight line? 720
	2) How many ways can we award a first and second place prize among eight contestants? 56
	3) In how many ways can we choose 4 players from a team of 10 players? 210

Topic	**Function Notation and Evaluation**
Notes	✓ Functions are mathematical operations that assign unique outputs to given inputs. ✓ Function notation is the way a function is written. It is meant to be a precise way of giving information about the function without a rather lengthy written explanation. ✓ The most popular function notation is $f(x)$ which is read "f of x". ✓ To evaluate a function, plug in the input (the given value or expression) for the function's variable (place holder, x).
Example	**Evaluate**: $h(n) = 2n^2 - 2$, find $h(2)$. **Solution:** Substitute n with 2: Then: $h(n) = 2n^2 - 2 \rightarrow h(2) = 2(2)^2 - 2 = 8 - 2 \rightarrow h(2) = 6$

Your Turn!	1) $f(x) = x - 1$, find $f(-2)$ _____	2) $g(x) = 3x + 2$, find $g(2)$ _____
	3) $g(n) = 2n - 8$, find $g(-1)$ _____	4) $h(n) = n^2 - 1$, find $h(-2)$ _____
Find more at bit.ly/3mIs7lF	5) $f(x) = x^2 + 12$, find $f(5)$ _____	6) $g(x) = 2x^2 - 9$, find $g(-2)$_____
	7) $w(x) = 3x^2 - x$, find $w(2n)$ _____	8) $p(x) = 2x^3 - 8$, find $p(-2a)$ _____

Topic	Function Notation and Evaluation – Answers
Notes	✓ Functions are mathematical operations that assign unique outputs to given inputs. ✓ Function notation is the way a function is written. It is meant to be a precise way of giving information about the function without a rather lengthy written explanation. ✓ The most popular function notation is $f(x)$ which is read "f of x". ✓ To evaluate a function, plug in the input (the given value or expression) for the function's variable (place holder, x).
Example	**Evaluate**: $h(n) = 2n^2 - 2$, find $h(2)$. **Solution:** Substitute n with 2: Then: $h(n) = 2n^2 - 2 \rightarrow h(2) = 2(2)^2 - 2 = 8 - 2 \rightarrow h(2) = 6$

Your Turn!	1) $f(x) = x - 1$, find $f(-2)$ $f(-2) = -3$	2) $g(x) = 3x + 2$, find $g(2)$ $g(2) = 8$
	3) $g(n) = 2n - 8$, find $g(-1)$ $g(-1) = -10$	4) $h(n) = n^2 - 1$, find $h(-2)$ $h(-2) = 3$
Find more at bit.ly/3mIs7lF	5) $f(x) = x^2 + 12$, find $f(5)$ $f(5) = 37$	6) $g(x) = 2x^2 - 9$, find $g(-2)$ $g(-2) = -1$
	7) $w(x) = 3x^2 - x$, find $w(2n)$ $w(3n) = 12n^2 - 2n$	8) $p(x) = 2x^3 - 8$, find $p(-2a)$ $p(-2a) = -16a^3 - 8$

Topic	Adding and Subtracting Functions
Notes	✓ Just like we can add and subtract numbers and expressions, we can add or subtract two functions and simplify or evaluate them. The result is a new function. ✓ For two functions $f(x)$ and $g(x)$, we can create two new functions: $(f + g)(x) = f(x) + g(x)$ and $(f - g)(x) = f(x) - g(x)$
Example	$g(a) = 2a - 5$, $f(a) = a + 8$, **Find**: $(g + f)(a)$ **Solution:** $(g + f)(a) = g(a) + f(a)$ Then: $(g + f)(a) = (2a - 5) + (a + 8) = 3a + 3$

Your Turn!		
	1) $g(x) = x - 3$ $h(x) = 2x + 5$ Find: $(h + g)(2)$ ____	2) $f(x) = 2x + 6$ $g(x) = -x - 5$ Find: $(f + g)(3)$ ____
	3) $f(x) = 5x + 8$ $g(x) = 3x - 12$ Find: $(f - g)(-2)$ ____	4) $h(x) = 2x^2 - 10$ $g(x) = 3x + 12$ Find: $(h + g)(3)$ ____
Find more at bit.ly/3hdeFVO	5) $g(x) = 10x - 7$ $h(x) = 3x^2 + 11$ Find: $(h - g)(x)$ ____	6) $h(x) = -x^2 - 15$ $g(x) = 3x^2 + 18$ Find: $(h - g)(a)$ ____

Topic	Adding and Subtracting Functions – Answers
Notes	✓ Just like we can add and subtract numbers and expressions, we can add or subtract two functions and simplify or evaluate them. The result is a new function. ✓ For two functions $f(x)$ and $g(x)$, we can create two new functions: $(f + g)(x) = f(x) + g(x)$ and $(f - g)(x) = f(x) - g(x)$
Example	$g(a) = 2a - 5$, $f(a) = a + 8$, Find: $(g + f)(a)$ **Solution:** $(g + f)(a) = g(a) + f(a)$ Then: $(g + f)(a) = (2a - 5) + (a + 8) = 3a + 3$

Your Turn!		
	1) $g(x) = x - 3$ $h(x) = 2x + 5$ Find: $(h + g)(2)$ 8	2) $f(x) = 2x + 6$ $g(x) = -x - 5$ Find: $(f + g)(3)$ 4
	3) $f(x) = 5x + 8$ $g(x) = 3x - 12$ Find: $(f - g)(-2)$ 16	4) $h(x) = 2x^2 - 10$ $g(x) = 3x + 12$ Find: $(h + g)(3)$ 29
Find more at bit.ly/3hdeFVO	5) $g(x) = 10x - 7$ $h(x) = 3x^2 + 11$ Find: $(h - g)(x)$ $3x^2 - 10x + 18$	6) $h(x) = -x^2 - 15$ $g(x) = 3x^2 + 18$ Find: $(h - g)(a)$ $-4a^2 - 33$

Topic	**Multiplying and Dividing Functions**
Notes	✓ Just like we can multiply and divide numbers and expressions, we can multiply and divide two functions and simplify or evaluate them. ✓ For two functions $f(x)$ and $g(x)$, we can create two new functions: $(f.g)(x) = f(x).g(x)$ and $\left(\frac{f}{g}\right)(x) = \frac{f(x)}{g(x)}$
Example	$g(x) = x + 5, f(x) = x - 3$, Find: $(g.f)(2)$ **Solution:** $(g.f)(x) = g(x).f(x) = (x+5)(x-3) = x^2 - 3x + 5x - 15 = x^2 + 2x - 15$ Substitute x with 2: $(g.f)(x) = (2)^2 + 2(2) - 15 = 4 + 4 - 15 = -7$

Your Turn!	1) $g(x) = x - 1$ $h(x) = x + 2$ Find: $(g.h)(-3)$ _____	2) $f(x) = x + 2$ $g(x) = -x - 3$ Find: $(\frac{f}{g})(-4)$ _____
	3) $f(x) = 5x + 3$ $g(x) = 2x - 4$ Find: $(\frac{f}{g})(5)$ _____	4) $h(x) = x^2 - 2$ $g(x) = x + 4$ Find: $(g.h)(3)$ _____
Find more at bit.ly/3ph7kHA	5) $g(x) = 2x - 8$ $h(x) = x^2 + 6$ Find: $(g.h)(-2)$ _____	6) $h(x) = 3x^2 - 8$ $g(x) = 4x + 3$ Find: $(\frac{h}{g})(-1)$ _____

Topic	Multiplying and Dividing Functions - Answers
Notes	✓ Just like we can multiply and divide numbers and expressions, we can multiply and divide two functions and simplify or evaluate them. ✓ For two functions $f(x)$ and $g(x)$, we can create two new functions: $(f.g)(x) = f(x).g(x)$ and $\left(\frac{f}{g}\right)(x) = \frac{f(x)}{g(x)}$
Example	$g(x) = x + 5, f(x) = x - 3$, Find: $(g.f)(2)$ **Solution:** $(g.f)(x) = g(x).f(x) = (x+5)(x-3) = x^2 - 3x + 5x - 15 = x^2 + 2x - 15$ Substitute x with 2: $(g.f)(x) = (2)^2 + 2(2) - 15 = 4 + 4 - 15 = -7$
Your Turn!	1) $g(x) = x - 1$ $h(x) = x + 2$ Find: $(g.h)(-3)$ $(g.h)(-3) = 4$	2) $f(x) = x + 2$ $g(x) = -x - 3$ Find: $\left(\frac{f}{g}\right)(-4)$ $\left(\frac{f}{g}\right)(-4) = -2$

	3) $f(x) = 5x + 3$ $g(x) = 2x - 4$ Find: $\left(\frac{f}{g}\right)(5)$ $\left(\frac{f}{g}\right)(5) = \frac{14}{3}$	4) $h(x) = x^2 - 2$ $g(x) = x + 4$ Find: $(g.h)(3)$ $(g.h)(3) = 49$
Find more at bit.ly/3ph7kHA 	5) $g(x) = 2x - 8$ $h(x) = x^2 + 6$ Find: $(g.h)(-2)$ $(g.h)(-2) = -120$	6) $h(x) = 3x^2 - 8$ $g(x) = 4x + 3$ Find: $\left(\frac{h}{g}\right)(-1)$ $\left(\frac{h}{g}\right)(-1) = 5$

Topic	Composition of Functions
Notes	✓ "Composition of functions" simply means combining two or more functions in a way where the output from one function becomes the input for the next function. ✓ The notation used for composition is: $(f o g)(x) = f(g(x))$ and is read "f composed with g of x" or "f of g of x".
Example	**Using** $f(x) = x - 8$ **and** $g(x) = x + 2$, **find**: $(f \ o \ g)(3)$ **Solution:** $(f \ o \ g)(x) = f(g(x))$ **Then:** $(f \ o \ g)(x) = f(g(x)) = f(x + 2) = x + 2 - 8 = x - 6$ Substitute x with 3: $(f \ o \ g)(3) = f(g(3)) = 3 - 6 = -3$
Your Turn! **Find more at** bit.ly/2WHBkAg	1) $f(x) = 3x$ $g(x) = x + 2$ Find: $(fog)(2)$ _____ ‖ 2) $f(x) = x + 3$ $g(x) = x - 1$ Find: $(fog)(-2)$ _____ 3) $f(x) = 3x$ $g(x) = x + 4$ Find: $(gof)(4)$ _____ ‖ 4) $h(x) = 2x - 2$ $g(x) = x + 4$ Find: $(goh)(2)$ _____ 5) $f(x) = 3x - 1$ $g(x) = x + 8$ Find: $(fog)(-1)$ _____ ‖ 6) $f(x) = x^2 - 4$ $g(x) = 3x + 1$ Find: $(gof)(2)$ _____

Topic	Composition of Functions – Answers
Notes	✓ "Composition of functions" simply means combining two or more functions in a way where the output from one function becomes the input for the next function. ✓ The notation used for composition is: $(f o g)(x) = f(g(x))$ and is read "f composed with g of x" or "f of g of x".
Example	**Using** $f(x) = x - 8$ **and** $g(x) = x + 2$, **find:** $(f \ o \ g)(3)$ **Solution:** $(f \ o \ g)(x) = f(g(x))$ *Then:* $(f \ o \ g)(x) = f(g(x)) = f(x + 2) = x + 2 - 8 = x - 6$ Substitute x with 3: $(f \ o \ g)(3) = f(g(3)) = 3 - 6 = -3$

Your Turn!	1) $f(x) = 3x$ $g(x) = x + 2$ Find: $(fog)(2)$ 12	2) $f(x) = x + 3$ $g(x) = x - 1$ Find: $(fog)(-2)$ 0
	3) $f(x) = 3x$ $g(x) = x + 4$ Find: $(gof)(4)$ 16	4) $h(x) = 2x - 2$ $g(x) = x + 4$ Find: $(goh)(2)$ 6
Find more at bit.ly/2WHBkAg	5) $f(x) = 3x - 1$ $g(x) = x + 8$ Find: $(fog)(-1)$ 20	6) $f(x) = x^2 - 4$ $g(x) = 3x + 1$ Find: $(gof)(2)$ 1

Time to test

Time to refine your Math skill with a practice examination

Take a practice HiSET Math Test to simulate the test day experience. After you've finished, score your test using the answer key.

Before You Start

- You'll need a pencil and a calculator to take the test.

- All questions are multiple choice questions. There are five possible answers for each question. Choose which one is best.

- It's okay to guess. You won't lose any points if you're wrong.

- The HiSET Mathematics test contains a formula sheet, which displays formulas relating to geometric measurement and certain algebra concepts. Formulas are provided to test-takers so that they may focus on application, rather than the memorization, of formulas.

- After you've finished the test, review the answer key to see where you went wrong and what areas you need to improve.

Good luck!

HiSET Mathematics

Practice Test 1

2022-2023

Total number of questions: 55

Total time (Calculator): 90 Minutes

Calculators are permitted for HiSET Math Test.

HiSET Mathematics Practice Tests Answer Sheet

Remove (or photocopy) this answer sheet and use it to complete the practice test.

HiSET Mathematics Practice Test 1 Answer Sheet

1	Ⓐ Ⓑ Ⓒ Ⓓ Ⓔ	21	Ⓐ Ⓑ Ⓒ Ⓓ Ⓔ
2	Ⓐ Ⓑ Ⓒ Ⓓ Ⓔ	22	Ⓐ Ⓑ Ⓒ Ⓓ Ⓔ
3	Ⓐ Ⓑ Ⓒ Ⓓ Ⓔ	23	Ⓐ Ⓑ Ⓒ Ⓓ Ⓔ
4	Ⓐ Ⓑ Ⓒ Ⓓ Ⓔ	24	Ⓐ Ⓑ Ⓒ Ⓓ Ⓔ
5	Ⓐ Ⓑ Ⓒ Ⓓ Ⓔ	25	Ⓐ Ⓑ Ⓒ Ⓓ Ⓔ
6	Ⓐ Ⓑ Ⓒ Ⓓ Ⓔ	26	Ⓐ Ⓑ Ⓒ Ⓓ Ⓔ
7	Ⓐ Ⓑ Ⓒ Ⓓ Ⓔ	27	Ⓐ Ⓑ Ⓒ Ⓓ Ⓔ
8	Ⓐ Ⓑ Ⓒ Ⓓ Ⓔ	28	Ⓐ Ⓑ Ⓒ Ⓓ Ⓔ
9	Ⓐ Ⓑ Ⓒ Ⓓ Ⓔ	29	Ⓐ Ⓑ Ⓒ Ⓓ Ⓔ
10	Ⓐ Ⓑ Ⓒ Ⓓ Ⓔ	30	Ⓐ Ⓑ Ⓒ Ⓓ Ⓔ
11	Ⓐ Ⓑ Ⓒ Ⓓ Ⓔ	31	Ⓐ Ⓑ Ⓒ Ⓓ Ⓔ
12	Ⓐ Ⓑ Ⓒ Ⓓ Ⓔ	32	Ⓐ Ⓑ Ⓒ Ⓓ Ⓔ
13	Ⓐ Ⓑ Ⓒ Ⓓ Ⓔ	33	Ⓐ Ⓑ Ⓒ Ⓓ Ⓔ
14	Ⓐ Ⓑ Ⓒ Ⓓ Ⓔ	34	Ⓐ Ⓑ Ⓒ Ⓓ Ⓔ
15	Ⓐ Ⓑ Ⓒ Ⓓ Ⓔ	35	Ⓐ Ⓑ Ⓒ Ⓓ Ⓔ
16	Ⓐ Ⓑ Ⓒ Ⓓ Ⓔ	36	Ⓐ Ⓑ Ⓒ Ⓓ Ⓔ
17	Ⓐ Ⓑ Ⓒ Ⓓ Ⓔ	37	Ⓐ Ⓑ Ⓒ Ⓓ Ⓔ
18	Ⓐ Ⓑ Ⓒ Ⓓ Ⓔ	38	Ⓐ Ⓑ Ⓒ Ⓓ Ⓔ
19	Ⓐ Ⓑ Ⓒ Ⓓ Ⓔ	39	Ⓐ Ⓑ Ⓒ Ⓓ Ⓔ
20	Ⓐ Ⓑ Ⓒ Ⓓ Ⓔ	40	Ⓐ Ⓑ Ⓒ Ⓓ Ⓔ

41	Ⓐ Ⓑ Ⓒ Ⓓ Ⓔ
42	Ⓐ Ⓑ Ⓒ Ⓓ Ⓔ
43	Ⓐ Ⓑ Ⓒ Ⓓ Ⓔ
44	Ⓐ Ⓑ Ⓒ Ⓓ Ⓔ
45	Ⓐ Ⓑ Ⓒ Ⓓ Ⓔ
46	Ⓐ Ⓑ Ⓒ Ⓓ Ⓔ
47	Ⓐ Ⓑ Ⓒ Ⓓ Ⓔ
48	Ⓐ Ⓑ Ⓒ Ⓓ Ⓔ
49	Ⓐ Ⓑ Ⓒ Ⓓ Ⓔ
50	Ⓐ Ⓑ Ⓒ Ⓓ Ⓔ
51	Ⓐ Ⓑ Ⓒ Ⓓ Ⓔ
52	Ⓐ Ⓑ Ⓒ Ⓓ Ⓔ
53	Ⓐ Ⓑ Ⓒ Ⓓ Ⓔ
54	Ⓐ Ⓑ Ⓒ Ⓓ Ⓔ
55	Ⓐ Ⓑ Ⓒ Ⓓ Ⓔ

Formula Sheet

Perimeter / Circumference

Rectangle

$Perimeter = 2(length) + 2(width)$

Circle

$Circumference = 2\pi(radius)$

Area

Circle

$Area = \pi(radius)^2$

Triangle

$Area = \frac{1}{2}(base)(height)$

Parallelogram

$Area = (base)(height)$

Trapezoid

$Area = \frac{1}{2}(base_1 + base_2)(height)$

Volume

Prism/Cylinder

$Volume = (area\ of\ the\ base)(height)$

Pyramid/Cone

$Volume = \frac{1}{3}(area\ of\ the\ base)(height)$

Sphere

$Volume = \frac{4}{3}\pi(radius)^3$

Length

1 foot = 12 inches

1 yard = 3 feet

1 mile = 5,280 feet

1 meter = 1,000 millimeters

1 meter = 100 centimeters

1 kilometer = 1,000 meters

1 mile ≈ 1.6 kilometers

1 inch = 2.54 centimeters

1 foot ≈ 0.3 meter

Capacity / Volume

1 cup = 8 fluid ounces

1 pint = 2 cups

1 quart = 2 pints

1 gallon = 4 quarts

1 gallon = 231 cubic inches

1 liter = 1,000 milliliters

1 liter ≈ 0.264 gallon

Weight

1 pound = 16 ounces

1 ton = 2,000 pounds

1 gram = 1,000 milligrams

1 kilogram = 1,000 grams

1 kilogram ≈ 2.2 pounds

1 ounce ≈ 28.3 grams

1) What is the length of AB in the following figure if AE = 4, CD = 6 and AC = 12?

A. 3.8

B. 4.8

C. 7.2

D. 24

E. 48

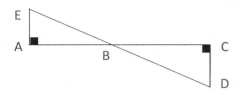

2) If the area of the following trapezoid is 126 cm, what is the perimeter of the trapezoid? (Figure not drawn to scale.)

A. 12 *cm*

B. 13 *cm*

C. 32 *cm*

D. 46 *cm*

E. 55 *cm*

3) If 5 *inches* on a map represents an actual distance of 100 feet, then, what actual distance does 18 inches on the map represent?

A. 18

B. 20

C. 100

D. 250

E. 360

4) Which of the following lists shows the fractions in order from least to greatest?

$$\frac{3}{4}, \frac{2}{7}, \frac{3}{8}, \frac{5}{11}$$

A. $\frac{3}{8}, \frac{2}{7}, \frac{3}{4}, \frac{5}{11}$

B. $\frac{3}{8}, \frac{2}{7}, \frac{5}{11}, \frac{3}{4}$

C. $\frac{2}{7}, \frac{5}{11}, \frac{3}{8}, \frac{3}{4}$

D. $\frac{2}{7}, \frac{3}{8}, \frac{5}{11}, \frac{3}{4}$

E. $\frac{5}{11}, \frac{3}{4}, \frac{3}{8}, \frac{2}{7}$

5) The following graph shows the mark of seven students in mathematics. What is the mean (average) of the marks?

A. 15

B. 14.5

C. 14

D. 13.5

E. 13

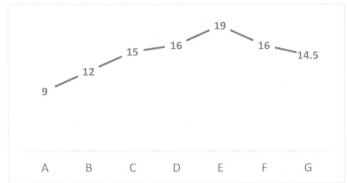

Questions 6 to 8 are based on the following data

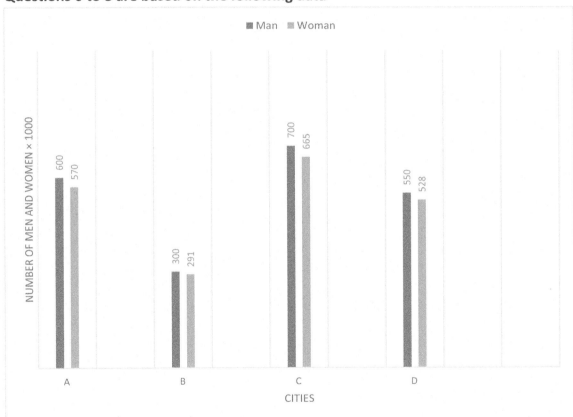

6) What's the maximum ratio of woman to man in the four cities?

A. 0.98

B. 0.97

C. 0.96

D. 0.95

E. 0.94

7) What's the ratio of percentage of men in city A to percentage of women in city C?

    A. 0.85

    B. 0.9

    C. 0.95

    D. 1

    E. 1.05

8) How many women should be added to city D until the ratio of women to men will be 1.2?

    A. 120

    B. 123

    C. 128

    D. 132

    E. 160

9) What is the value of 6^4?

    A. 6

    B. 24

    C. 36

    D. 216

    E. 1,296

10) How many $\frac{1}{5}$ pound paperback books together weigh 50 pounds?

    A. 25

    B. 50

    C. 150

    D. 200

    E. 250

11) What is the volume of the following square pyramid?

    A. $100 \, m^3$

    B. $120 \, m^3$

    C. $144 \, m^3$

    D. $480 \, m^3$

    E. $1,440 \, m^3$

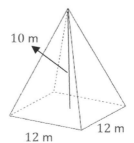

10 m

12 m   12 m

12 m

12) The surface area of a cylinder is 150π cm^2. If its height is 10 cm, what is the radius of the cylinder?

    A. 20 cm

    B. 15 cm

    C. 13 cm

    D. 11 cm

    E. 5 cm

13) In the following shape, the area of the circle is 16π. What is the area of the square?

    A. 4

    B. 8

    C. 16

    D. 32

    E. 64

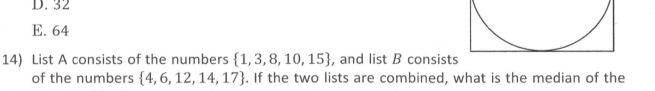

14) List A consists of the numbers $\{1, 3, 8, 10, 15\}$, and list B consists of the numbers $\{4, 6, 12, 14, 17\}$. If the two lists are combined, what is the median of the combined list?

    A. 9

    B. 10

    C. 12

    D. 15

    E. 17

15) What's the area of the non-shaded part of the following figure?

    A. 236

    B. 192

    C. 152

    D. 42

    E. 40

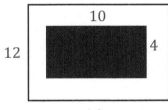

16) In the triangle below, if the measure of angle A is 37 degrees, then what is the value of y? (figure is NOT drawn to scale)

A. 37

B. 62

C. 70

D. 78

E. 86

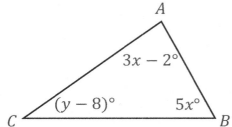

Questions 17 to 19 are based on the following data

Types of air pollutions in 10 cities of a country

Type of Pollution	Number of Cities									
A	■	■	■	■	■	■				
B	■	■	■							
C	■	■	■	■						
D	■	■	■	■	■	■	■	■	■	
E	■	■	■	■	■	■	■	■		
	1	2	3	4	5	6	7	8	9	10

17) If a is the mean (average) of the number of cities in each pollution type category, b is the mode, and c is the median of the number of cities in each pollution type category, then which of the following must be true?

A. $a < b < c$

B. $b < a < c$

C. $b < c < b$

D. $a = c$

E. $b < c = a$

18) What percent of cities are in the type of pollution A, C, and D respectively?

A. 60%, 40%, 90%

B. 40%, 90%, 60%

C. 40%, 60%, 90%

D. 30%, 40%, 90%

E. 30%, 40%, 60%

19) How many cities should be added to type of pollutions B until the ratio of cities in type of pollution B to cities in type of pollution E will be 0.625?

A. 2

B. 3

C. 4

D. 5

E. 6

20) There are only red and blue cards in a box. The probability of choosing a red card in the box at random is one third. If there are 246 blue cards, how many cards are in the box?

A. 123

B. 246

C. 308

D. 328

E. 369

21) $\frac{1}{6b^2} + \frac{1}{6b} = \frac{1}{b^2}$, then b = ?

A. $-\frac{15}{16}$

B. $-\frac{16}{15}$

C. 5

D. 6

E. 8

22) In the diagram below, circle A represents the set of all odd numbers, circle B represents the set of all negative numbers, and circle C represents the set of all multiples of 5. Which number could be replaced with y?

A. 0

B. 5

C. -5

D. 10

E. -10

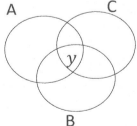

23) Which of the following graphs represents the compound inequality?
$$-2 \leq 2x - 4 < 2?$$

A.

B.

C.

D.

E.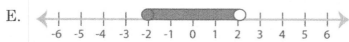

24) A basket contains 20 balls and the average weight of each of these balls is 25 g. The five heaviest balls have an average weight of 40 g each. If we remove the five heaviest balls from the basket, what is the average weight of the remaining balls?

A. 10

B. 20

C. 30

D. 35

E. 40

25) In a stadium the ratio of home fans to visiting fans in a crowd is 5 : 7. Which of the following could be the total number of fans in the stadium?

A. 12,324

B. 42,326

C. 44,566

D. 66,812

E. 69,752

26) What is the perimeter of a square in centimeters that has an area of 595.36 cm^2?

A. 97.6

B. 96.2

C. 95.7

D. 92.6

E. 90.3

27) A bread recipe calls for $2\frac{2}{3}$ cups of flour. If you only have $1\frac{5}{6}$ cups, how much more flour is needed?

   A. 1

   B. $2\frac{11}{6}$

   C. $\frac{1}{2}$

   D. $\frac{5}{6}$

   E. $\frac{11}{6}$

28) If $x = \frac{1}{3}$ and $y = \frac{9}{21}$, then which is equal to $\frac{1}{x} \div \frac{y}{3}$?

   A. $\frac{1}{7}$

   B. $\frac{1}{3}$

   C. $\frac{2}{3}$

   D. $\frac{1}{21}$

   E. 21

29) If Jim adds 100 stamps to his current stamp collection, the total number of stamps will be equal to $\frac{6}{5}$ the current number of stamps. If Jim adds 50% more stamps to the current collection, how many stamps will be in the collection?

   A. 150

   B. 300

   C. 500

   D. 600

   E. 750

30) The sum of 8 numbers is greater than 240 and less than 320. Which of the following could be the average (arithmetic mean) of the numbers?

   A. 25

   B. 30

   C. 35

   D. 40

   E. 45

31) In the following figure, point Q lies on line n, what is the value of y if $x = 35$?

   A. 15

   B. 25

   C. 30

   D. 35

   E. 45

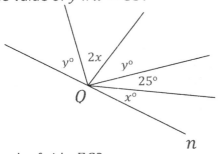

32) Triangle ABC is similar to triangle ADE. What is the length of side EC?

   A. 4.5

   B. 9

   C. 18

   D. 27

   E. 36

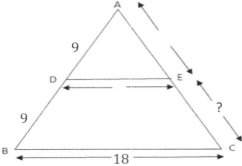

33) Ella (E) is 4 years older than her friend Ava (A) who is 3 years younger than her sister Sofia (S). If E, A and S denote their ages, which one of the following represents the given information?

   A. $\begin{cases} E = A + 4 \\ S = A - 3 \end{cases}$

   B. $\begin{cases} E = A + 4 \\ A = S + 3 \end{cases}$

   C. $\begin{cases} A = E + 4 \\ S = A - 3 \end{cases}$

   D. $\begin{cases} E = A + 4 \\ A = S - 3 \end{cases}$

   E. $\begin{cases} E = A + 3 \\ S = A + 4 \end{cases}$

34) **The length of a rectangle is 3 meters greater than 4 times its width. The perimeter of the rectangle is 36 meters. What is the area of the rectangle in meters?**

   A. 15

   B. 35

   C. 45

   D. 55

   E. 65

35) Find the value of x in the following diagram. (there are 2 supplementary angles in the diagram?

A. 23

B. 36

C. 47

D. 68

E. 90

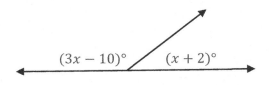

36) The circle graph below shows all Mr. Green's expenses for last month. If he spent $660 on his car, how much did he spend for his rent?

A. $660

B. $700

C. $740

D. $780

E. $810

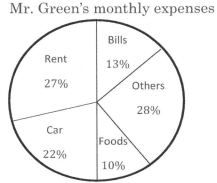

37) What is the area of the shaded region if the diameter of the bigger circle is 12 inches and the diameter of the smaller circle is 8 inches?

A. $16\pi\ in^2$

B. $20\pi\ in^2$

C. $36\pi\ in^2$

D. $48\pi\ in^2$

E. $80\pi\ in^2$

38) In the rectangle below if $y > 5\ cm$ and the area of rectangle is $50\ cm^2$ and the perimeter of the rectangle is $30\ cm$, what is the value of x and y?

A. $x = 15,\ y = 10$

B. $x = 15,\ y = 5$

C. $x = 10,\ y = 15$

D. $x = 10,\ y = 5$

E. $x = 5,\ y = 10$

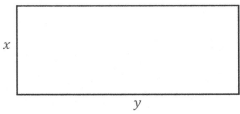

39) What is the value of x?

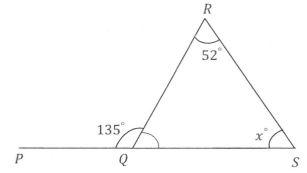

    A. 38

    B. 45

    C. 75

    D. 83

    E. 135

40) If x is directly proportional to the square of y, and $y = 2$ when $x = 12$, then when $x = 75$ $y = ?$

    A. $\frac{1}{5}$

    B. 1

    C. 5

    D. 12

    E. 25

41) Jack earns $616 for his first 44 hours of work in a week and is then paid 1.5 times his regular hourly rate for any additional hours. This week, Jack needs $826 to pay his rent, bills and other expenses. How many hours must he work to make enough money in this week?

    A. 40

    B. 43

    C. 48

    D. 54

    E. 62

42) What is 2.5% of 1,200?

    A. 900

    B. 600

    C. 300

    D. 60

    E. 30

43) If x is a real number, and if $x^3 + 18 = 130$, then x lies between which two consecutive integers?

   A. 1 and 2

   B. 2 and 3

   C. 3 and 4

   D. 4 and 5

   E. 5 and 6

44) Jack types 72 words per minute. How many words does he type in 15 seconds?

   A. 14

   B. 18

   C. 20

   D. 22

   E. 24

45) Which of the following is the same as: 0.000,000,000,000,042,121?

   A. 4.2121×10^{14}

   B. 4.2121×10^{13}

   C. 42.121×10^{-10}

   D. 42.121×10^{-13}

   E. 4.2121×10^{-14}

46) Which of the following is the largest?

   A. $|4 - 2|$

   B. $|2 - 4|$

   C. $|-2 - 4|$

   D. $|2 - 4| - |4 - 2|$

   E. $|2 - 4| + |4 - 2|$

47) A student gets 85% of a test with 40 questions. How many answers did the student solve correctly?

   A. 25

   B. 28

   C. 34

   D. 36

   E. 42

48) To buy a new computer, Emma borrowed $2,500 at 8% interest for 6 years. How much interest did she pay?

   A. $150

   B. $1,200

   C. $1,500

   D. $2,400

   E. $2,500

49) If n is an even integer that is less than -3.34, what is the greatest possible value of n?

   A. -1

   B. -2

   C. -3

   D. -4

   E. -5

50) Integer x is evenly divisible by 4. Which expression below is also evenly divisible by 4?

   A. $x + 1$

   B. $2x + 1$

   C. $2x + 4$

   D. $3x + 2$

   E. $4x + 1$

51) Sara has a box containing 5 blue balls, 8 red balls, and 3 green balls. If she removes one ball at random, what is the probability that it will not be blue?

   A. $\frac{1}{8}$

   B. $\frac{5}{16}$

   C. $\frac{5}{11}$

   D. $\frac{10}{11}$

   E. $\frac{11}{16}$

52) On the number line below, point M is located on line segment ON so that $OM = \frac{1}{3}MN$. What is the position of point M?

   A. -4.2

   B. -3.5

   C. -1.5

   D. 1.5

   E. 2.5

53) Jack rides 160 kilometers in 1 hour 20 minutes. At that rate, how many meters does he ride per minute?

   A. 1,000 meters

   B. 1,500 meters

   C. 1,600 meters

   D. 2,000 meters

   E. 2,500 meters

54) The sum of two consecutive integer is -13. If 2 is added to the smaller integer and 3 is subtract from the larger integer, what is the product of the two resulting integers?

   A. 5

   B. 9

   C. 18

   D. 28

   E. 45

55) A ladder leans against a wall forming a 60° angle between the ground and the ladder. If the bottom of the ladder is 30 feet away from the wall, how long is the ladder?

A. 30 *feet*

B. 40 *feet*

C. 50 *feet*

D. 60 *feet*

E. 120 *feet*

End of HiSET Mathematics Practice Test 1

HiSET Mathematics Practice Test 2

2022-2023

Total number of questions: 55

Total time (Calculator): 90 Minutes

Calculators are permitted for HiSET Math Test.

HiSET Mathematics Practice Tests Answer Sheet

Remove (or photocopy) this answer sheet and use it to complete the practice test.

HiSET Mathematics Practice Test 2 Answer Sheet

1 Ⓐ Ⓑ Ⓒ Ⓓ Ⓔ	21 Ⓐ Ⓑ Ⓒ Ⓓ Ⓔ	41 Ⓐ Ⓑ Ⓒ Ⓓ Ⓔ
2 Ⓐ Ⓑ Ⓒ Ⓓ Ⓔ	22 Ⓐ Ⓑ Ⓒ Ⓓ Ⓔ	42 Ⓐ Ⓑ Ⓒ Ⓓ Ⓔ
3 Ⓐ Ⓑ Ⓒ Ⓓ Ⓔ	23 Ⓐ Ⓑ Ⓒ Ⓓ Ⓔ	43 Ⓐ Ⓑ Ⓒ Ⓓ Ⓔ
4 Ⓐ Ⓑ Ⓒ Ⓓ Ⓔ	24 Ⓐ Ⓑ Ⓒ Ⓓ Ⓔ	44 Ⓐ Ⓑ Ⓒ Ⓓ Ⓔ
5 Ⓐ Ⓑ Ⓒ Ⓓ Ⓔ	25 Ⓐ Ⓑ Ⓒ Ⓓ Ⓔ	45 Ⓐ Ⓑ Ⓒ Ⓓ Ⓔ
6 Ⓐ Ⓑ Ⓒ Ⓓ Ⓔ	26 Ⓐ Ⓑ Ⓒ Ⓓ Ⓔ	46 Ⓐ Ⓑ Ⓒ Ⓓ Ⓔ
7 Ⓐ Ⓑ Ⓒ Ⓓ Ⓔ	27 Ⓐ Ⓑ Ⓒ Ⓓ Ⓔ	47 Ⓐ Ⓑ Ⓒ Ⓓ Ⓔ
8 Ⓐ Ⓑ Ⓒ Ⓓ Ⓔ	28 Ⓐ Ⓑ Ⓒ Ⓓ Ⓔ	48 Ⓐ Ⓑ Ⓒ Ⓓ Ⓔ
9 Ⓐ Ⓑ Ⓒ Ⓓ Ⓔ	29 Ⓐ Ⓑ Ⓒ Ⓓ Ⓔ	49 Ⓐ Ⓑ Ⓒ Ⓓ Ⓔ
10 Ⓐ Ⓑ Ⓒ Ⓓ Ⓔ	30 Ⓐ Ⓑ Ⓒ Ⓓ Ⓔ	50 Ⓐ Ⓑ Ⓒ Ⓓ Ⓔ
11 Ⓐ Ⓑ Ⓒ Ⓓ Ⓔ	31 Ⓐ Ⓑ Ⓒ Ⓓ Ⓔ	51 Ⓐ Ⓑ Ⓒ Ⓓ Ⓔ
12 Ⓐ Ⓑ Ⓒ Ⓓ Ⓔ	32 Ⓐ Ⓑ Ⓒ Ⓓ Ⓔ	52 Ⓐ Ⓑ Ⓒ Ⓓ Ⓔ
13 Ⓐ Ⓑ Ⓒ Ⓓ Ⓔ	33 Ⓐ Ⓑ Ⓒ Ⓓ Ⓔ	53 Ⓐ Ⓑ Ⓒ Ⓓ Ⓔ
14 Ⓐ Ⓑ Ⓒ Ⓓ Ⓔ	34 Ⓐ Ⓑ Ⓒ Ⓓ Ⓔ	54 Ⓐ Ⓑ Ⓒ Ⓓ Ⓔ
15 Ⓐ Ⓑ Ⓒ Ⓓ Ⓔ	35 Ⓐ Ⓑ Ⓒ Ⓓ Ⓔ	55 Ⓐ Ⓑ Ⓒ Ⓓ Ⓔ
16 Ⓐ Ⓑ Ⓒ Ⓓ Ⓔ	36 Ⓐ Ⓑ Ⓒ Ⓓ Ⓔ	
17 Ⓐ Ⓑ Ⓒ Ⓓ Ⓔ	37 Ⓐ Ⓑ Ⓒ Ⓓ Ⓔ	
18 Ⓐ Ⓑ Ⓒ Ⓓ Ⓔ	38 Ⓐ Ⓑ Ⓒ Ⓓ Ⓔ	
19 Ⓐ Ⓑ Ⓒ Ⓓ Ⓔ	39 Ⓐ Ⓑ Ⓒ Ⓓ Ⓔ	
20 Ⓐ Ⓑ Ⓒ Ⓓ Ⓔ	40 Ⓐ Ⓑ Ⓒ Ⓓ Ⓔ	

Formula Sheet

Perimeter / Circumference

Rectangle

$Perimeter = 2(length) + 2(width)$

Circle

$Circumference = 2\pi(radius)$

Area

Circle

$Area = \pi(radius)^2$

Triangle

$Area = \frac{1}{2}(base)(height)$

Parallelogram

$Area = (base)(height)$

Trapezoid

$Area = \frac{1}{2}(base_1 + base_2)(height)$

Volume

Prism/Cylinder

$Volume = (area\ of\ the\ base)(height)$

Pyramid/Cone

$Volume = \frac{1}{3}(area\ of\ the\ base)(height)$

Sphere

$Volume = \frac{4}{3}\pi(radius)^3$

Length

1 foot = 12 inches

1 yard = 3 feet

1 mile = 5,280 feet

1 meter = 1,000 millimeters

1 meter = 100 centimeters

1 kilometer = 1,000 meters

1 mile ≈ 1.6 kilometers

1 inch = 2.54 centimeters

1 foot ≈ 0.3 meter

Capacity / Volume

1 cup = 8 fluid ounces

1 pint = 2 cups

1 quart = 2 pints

1 gallon = 4 quarts

1 gallon = 231 cubic inches

1 liter = 1,000 milliliters

1 liter ≈ 0.264 gallon

Weight

1 pound = 16 ounces

1 ton = 2,000 pounds

1 gram = 1,000 milligrams

1 kilogram = 1,000 grams

1 kilogram ≈ 2.2 pounds

1 ounce ≈ 28.3 grams

1) The capacity of a red box is 20% bigger than the capacity of a blue box. If the red box can hold 30 equal sized books, how many of the same books can the blue box hold?

   A. 9

   B. 15

   C. 21

   D. 25

   E. 30

2) Kim spent $35 for pants. This was $10 less than triple what she spent for a shirt. How much was the shirt?

   A. $11

   B. $13

   C. $15

   D. $17

   E. $21

3) What is the greatest integer less than $-\frac{32}{5}$?

   A. 0

   B. -2

   C. -4

   D. -6

   E. -7

4) The measure of the angles of a triangle are in the ratio $1:3:5$. What is the measure of the largest angle?

   A. $20°$

   B. $45°$

   C. $85°$

   D. $100°$

   E. $180°$

5) In the figure below, line A is parallel to line B. what is the value of x?

A. 28

B. 46

C. 50

D. 55

E. 65

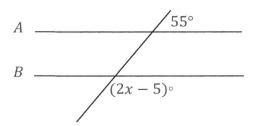

6) The mean of 50 test scores was calculated as 85. But it turned out that one of the scores was misread as 94 but it was 69. What is the mean?

A. 84.5

B. 87

C. 87.5

D. 88.5

E. 90.5

7) Which of the following answers represents the compound inequality?
$-4 \leq 4x - 8 < 16$?

A. $-2 \leq x \leq 8$

B. $-2 < x \leq 8$

C. $1 < x \leq 6$

D. $1 \leq x < 6$

E. $2 \leq x \leq 6$

8) In the following figure, $ABCD$ is a rectangle. If $a = \sqrt{3}$, and $b = 2a$, find the area of the shaded region. (the shaded region is a trapezoid)

A. $2\sqrt{3}$

B. $3\sqrt{3}$

C. $4\sqrt{3}$

D. $6\sqrt{3}$

E. $8\sqrt{3}$

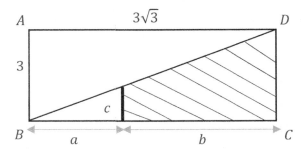

9) Which graph shows a non-proportional linear relationship between x and y?

A.
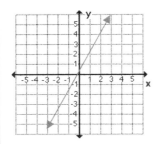

B.
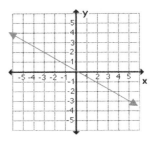

C.
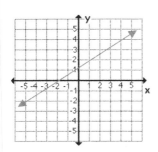

D.
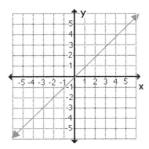

E.
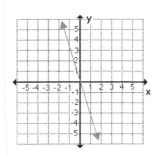

10) In the figure below, what is the value of x?

A. 8

B. 11

C. 15

D. 16

E. 32

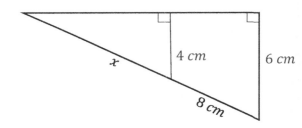

11) Anna opened an account with a deposit of $3,000. This account earns 5% simple interest annually. How many years will it take her to earn $600 on her $3,000 deposit?

   A. 2

   B. 4

   C. 5

   D. 6

   E. 8

12) Tom picked $2\frac{2}{5}$ baskets of apples, and Sam picked $1\frac{3}{4}$ baskets of apples. How many baskets total did they pick?

   A. $1\frac{2}{3}$

   B. $2\frac{1}{12}$

   C. $3\frac{20}{23}$

   D. $4\frac{3}{20}$

   E. $5\frac{1}{12}$

13) A list of consecutive integers begins with k and ends with n. If $n - k = 46$, how many integers are in the list?

   A. 23

   B. 38

   C. 46

   D. 47

   E. 58

14) A piece of paper that is $2\frac{3}{5}$ feet long is cut into 2 pieces of different lengths. The shorter piece has a length of x feet. Which inequality expresses all possible values of x?

   A. $x < 2\frac{1}{10}$

   B. $x > 2$

   C. $x < 2\frac{3}{5}$

   D. $x > 1\frac{3}{10}$

   E. $x < 1\frac{3}{10}$

15) In an academy, course grades range from 0 to 100. Anna took 5 courses and her mean course grade was 80. William took 8 courses. If both students have the same sum of course grades, what was William's mean?

    A. 50

    B. 65

    C. 70

    D. 80

    E. 85

16) The sum of the numbers x, y, and z is 69. The ratio of x to y is $1:3$ and the ratio of y to z is $2:5$. What is the value of y?

    A. 9.6

    B. 15

    C. 18

    D. 21.6

    E. 33

17) Which number line below shows the solution to the inequality $-1 < \frac{x}{3} < 2$?

    A.

    B.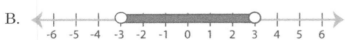

    C.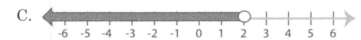

    D.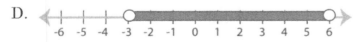

    E.

18) The set S consists of all odd numbers greater than 5 and less than 30. What is the mean of the numbers in S.

    A. 11

    B. 13

    C. 17

    D. 18

    E. 23

19) If $\sqrt{2y} = \sqrt{5x}$ then $x = \cdots$

 A. $\frac{1}{6}y$

 B. $\frac{1}{5}y$

 C. $\frac{2}{5}y$

 D. $\frac{5}{2}y$

 E. $10y$

20) A line connects the midpoint of AB (point E), with point C in the square $ABCD$. Calculate the area of the acquired trapezoid shape if the square has a side of $4\ m$.

 A. $4\ cm^2$

 B. $12\ cm^2$

 C. $15\ cm^2$

 D. $18\ cm^2$

 E. $24\ cm^2$

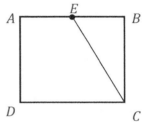

21) In a group of 45 student, 60% can't swim. How many students can swim?

 A. 13

 B. 18

 C. 22

 D. 23

 E. 35

22) $8,400 are distributed equally among 14 person. How much money will each person get?

 A. $400

 B. $450

 C. $584

 D. $600

 E. $800

23) A box contains 6 green sticks, 4 blue sticks, and 2 yellow sticks. Emma picks one without looking. What is the probability that the stick will be green?

A. $\frac{1}{2}$

B. $\frac{1}{3}$

C. $\frac{1}{4}$

D. $\frac{2}{5}$

E. $\frac{3}{2}$

24) The figure below, a square is inscribed in a circle. Calculate the shaded area in the figure below. Knowing that the radius of the circle is $6\ cm$. ($\pi = 3.14$)

A. $73.65\ cm^2$

B. $69.90\ cm^2$

C. $72.69\ cm^2$

D. $88.04\ cm^2$

E. $113.4\ cm^2$

25) The price of a Chocolate was raised from $5.40 to $5.67. What was the percent increase in the price?

A. 4%

B. 5%

C. 6%

D. 8%

E. 10%

26) In a box of blue and black marbles, the ratio of blue marbles to black marbles is $4:3$. If the box contains 150 black marbles, how many blue marbles are there?

A. 100

B. 150

C. 200

D. 300

E. 600

27) $\frac{5}{8}$ of a number is 90. Find the number.

   A. 144

   B. 270

   C. 450

   D. 720

   E. 800

28) A juice mixture contains $\frac{5}{14}$ jar of cherry juice and $\frac{5}{70}$ jar of apple juice. How many jars of cherry juice per jar of apple juice does the mixture contain?

   A. 70

   B. 14

   C. 10

   D. 7

   E. 5

29) In the figure below, $LMNO$ and $JMPQ$ are squares. Point O is the center of the circle, and points L and N are on the circle. If the area of the square is 16 square centimeters, what is the area, in square centimeters, of the shaded part?
   ($\pi = 3.14$)

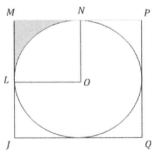

   A. 3

   B. 3.44

   C. 12

   D. 12.56

   E. 16

30) The set of possible values of n is $\{5, 3, 7\}$. What is the set of possible values of m if $2m = n + 5$?

   A. $\{2, 4, 7\}$

   B. $\{3, 2, 5\}$

   C. $\{4, 5, 8\}$

   D. $\{5, 4, 6\}$

   E. $\{6, 5, 8\}$

31) If $x = 25$, then which of the following equations are correct?

  A. $x + 10 = 40$

  B. $4x = 100$

  C. $3x = 70$

  D. $\frac{x}{2} = 12$

  E. $\frac{x}{3} = 8$

32) Jack scored a mean of 80 per test in his first 4 tests. In his 5th test, he scored 90. What was Jack's mean score for the 5 tests?

  A. 70

  B. 75

  C. 80

  D. 82

  E. 93

33) The volume of a cube is less than $64\ m^3$. Which of the following can be the cube's side?

  A. $2\ m$

  B. $4\ m$

  C. $8\ m$

  D. $10\ m$

  E. $11\ m$

34) What is the area of an isosceles right triangle that has one leg that measures $6\ cm$?

  A. $6\ cm^2$

  B. $12\ cm^2$

  C. $18\ cm^2$

  D. $24\ cm^2$

  E. $36\ cm^2$

35) If $0.00104 = \frac{104}{x}$, what is the value of x?

   A. 1,000

   B. 10,000

   C. 100,000

   D. 1,000,000

   E. 10,000,000

36) A bag is filled with numbered cards from 1 to 15 and picked on at random. What is the probability that the card picked is number 8?

   A. $\frac{8}{15}$

   B. $\frac{7}{15}$

   C. $\frac{5}{15}$

   D. $\frac{2}{15}$

   E. $\frac{1}{15}$

37) In the xy-plane, the point (4,3) and (3,2) are on line A. Which of the following points could also be on line A?

   A. $(5,7)$

   B. $(3,4)$

   C. $(-1,2)$

   D. $(-1,-2)$

   E. $(-7,-9)$

38) If $f(x)=2x^3+ 5x^2+ 2x$ and $g(x)= -2$, what is the value of $f(g(x))$?

   A. 36

   B. 32

   C. 24

   D. 4

   E. 0

39) What is the value of x in the figure below?

A. 32

B. 46

C. 54

D. 63

E. 76

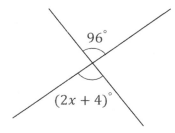

40) How many different two-digit numbers can be formed from the digits $6, 7$, and 5, if the numbers must be even and no digit can be repeated?

A. 1

B. 2

C. 3

D. 4

E. 5

41) A rectangular concrete driveway is 25 feet long, 6 feet wide, and 24 inches thick. What is the volume of the concrete?

A. $300\ ft^3$

B. $600\ ft^3$

C. $660\ ft^3$

D. $963\ ft^3$

E. $1,800\ ft^3$

42) If $\dfrac{2y}{x} - \dfrac{y}{3x} = \dfrac{(\ldots)}{3x}$ and $x \neq 0$, what expression is represented by $(\ldots)$?

A. $2y + 4$

B. $3y - 6$

C. $5y$

D. $6y$

E. $8y$

43) $200(3 + 0.01)^2 - 200 =$

    A. 201.55

    B. 361.08

    C. 702.88

    D. 1,612.02

    E. 1,812.02

44) If $360\ kg$ of vegetables is packed in 90 boxes, how much vegetables will each box contain?

    A. $2.5\ kg$

    B. $3\ kg$

    C. $4\ kg$

    D. $6.5\ kg$

    E. $7\ kg$

45) Each number in a sequence is 4 more than twice the number that comes just before it. If 84 is a number in the sequence, what number comes just before it?

    A. 26

    B. 35

    C. 40

    D. 52

    E. 88

46) $[6 \times (-24) + 8] - (-4) + [4 \times 5] \div 2 = ?$

    A. 148

    B. 132

    C. -122

    D. -136

    E. -144

47) Solve for x: $2 + \frac{3x}{x-5} = \frac{3}{5-x}$?

    A. $\frac{4}{5}$

    B. $\frac{6}{5}$

    C. $\frac{7}{5}$

    D. $\frac{8}{5}$

    E. $\frac{9}{5}$

48) A rectangle has 14 cm wide and 5 cm length. What is the perimeter of this rectangle?

    A. 29 cm

    B. 38 cm

    C. 43 cm

    D. 49 cm

    E. 58 cm

49) What is the value of the following expression? $3\frac{1}{4} + 2\frac{4}{16} + 1\frac{3}{8} + 5\frac{1}{2}$

    A. $3\frac{10}{14}$

    B. $4\frac{1}{2}$

    C. $12\frac{4}{16}$

    D. $12\frac{3}{8}$

    E. $12\frac{4}{8}$

50) A certain insect has a mass of 85 milligrams. What is the insect's mass in grams?

    A. 0.085

    B. 0.08

    C. 0.85

    D. 8.5

    E. 85

51) Removing which of the following numbers will change the average of the numbers to 6?

$$1, 4, 5, 8, 11, 12$$

    A. 1

    B. 4

    C. 5

    D. 8

    E. 11

52) If $m = 6$ and $n = -3$, what is the value of $\frac{5-9(3+n)}{3m-5(2-n)} = ?$

    A. $\frac{2}{7}$

    B. $\frac{3}{7}$

    C. $-\frac{4}{7}$

    D. $\frac{5}{7}$

    E. $-\frac{5}{7}$

53) Clara has 28 cookies. She is inviting 7 friends to a party. How many cookies will each friend get?

    A. 2

    B. 4

    C. 7

    D. 8

    E. 21

54) How long will it take to receive $360 in investment of $240 at the rate of 10% simple interest?

    A. 9 years

    B. 15 years

    C. 18 years

    D. 21 years

    E. 24 years

55) How many hours are there in 1,800 minutes?

   A. 20 hours

   B. 25 hours

   C. 30 hours

   D. 33 hours

   E. 60 hours

End of HiSET Mathematics Practice Test 2

HiSET Mathematics Practice Tests Answer Keys

Now, it's time to review your results to see where you went wrong and what areas you need to improve.

HiSET Practice Test 1						HiSET Practice Test 2					
1	B	21	C	41	D	1	D	21	B	41	A
2	D	22	C	42	E	2	C	22	D	42	C
3	E	23	D	43	D	3	E	23	A	43	D
4	D	24	B	44	B	4	D	24	D	44	C
5	B	25	A	45	E	5	E	25	B	45	C
6	B	26	A	46	C	6	A	26	C	46	C
7	E	27	D	47	C	7	D	27	A	47	C
8	D	28	E	48	B	8	C	28	E	48	B
9	E	29	E	49	D	9	C	29	B	49	D
10	E	30	C	50	C	10	D	30	D	50	A
11	D	31	B	51	E	11	B	31	B	51	E
12	E	32	B	52	B	12	D	32	D	52	E
13	E	33	D	53	D	13	D	33	B	53	B
14	A	34	C	54	E	14	E	34	C	54	B
15	C	35	C	55	D	15	A	35	C	55	C
16	E	36	E			16	C	36	E		
17	D	37	B			17	D	37	D		
18	A	38	E			18	D	38	E		
19	A	39	D			19	C	39	B		
20	E	40	C			20	B	40	B		

HiSET Mathematics Practice Test 1 Explanations

1) Choice B is correct

Two triangles ΔBAE and ΔBCD are similar. Then:

$\dfrac{AE}{CD} = \dfrac{AB}{BC} \rightarrow \dfrac{4}{6} = \dfrac{x}{12 - x} \rightarrow 48 - 4x = 6x \rightarrow 10x = 48 \rightarrow x = 4.8$

2) Choice D is correct

The area of the trapezoid is:

$Area = \dfrac{1}{2} h(b_1 + b_2) \rightarrow 126 = \dfrac{1}{2}(x)(13 + 8) \rightarrow 126 = 10.5x \rightarrow x = 12$

$y = \sqrt{5^2 + 12^2} = \sqrt{25 + 144} = \sqrt{169} = 13$

The perimeter of the trapezoid is: $12 + 13 + 8 + 13 = 46$

3) Choice E is correct

First calculate the number of feet that 1 inch represents: $100\ ft \div 5\ in = 20\ ft/in$

Then multiply this by the total number of inches: $18\ in \times 20\ ft/in = 360\ ft$

4) Choice D is correct

Let's compare each fraction: $\dfrac{2}{7} < \dfrac{3}{8} < \dfrac{5}{11} < \dfrac{3}{4}$

Only choice D provides the right order.

5) Choice B is correct

Use the average formula:

$average\ (mean) = \dfrac{sum\ of\ terms}{number\ of\ terms} = \dfrac{9 + 12 + 15 + 16 + 19 + 16 + 14.5}{7} = 14.5$

6) Choice B is correct

Ratio of women to men in city A: $\dfrac{570}{600} = 0.95$

Ratio of women to men in city B: $\dfrac{291}{300} = 0.97$

Ratio of women to men in city C: $\dfrac{665}{700} = 0.95$

Ratio of women to men in city D: $\dfrac{528}{550} = 0.96$

Choice B is the maximum number.

7) Choice E is correct

Percentage of men in city $A = \frac{600}{1,170} \times 100 = 51.28\%$

Percentage of women in city $C = \frac{665}{1,365} \times 100 = 48.72\%$

Percentage of men in city A to percentage of women in city $C = \frac{51.28}{48.72} = 1.05$

(Notice that $\frac{51.28}{48.72}$ is bigger than 1 and only choice E is bigger than 1)

8) Choice D is correct

Let the number of women should be added to city D be x, then:

$\frac{528+x}{550} = 1.2 \rightarrow 528 + x = 550 \times 1.2 \rightarrow x = 132$

9) Choice E is correct

$6^4 = 6 \times 6 \times 6 \times 6 = 1,296$

10) Choice E is correct

If each book weighs $\frac{1}{5}$ pound, then 1 pound = 5 books. To find the number of books in 50 pounds, simply multiply this 5 by 50: $50 \times 5 = 250$

11) Choice D is correct

Use the volume of square pyramid formula.

$V = \frac{1}{3}a^2h \Rightarrow V = \frac{1}{3}(12\,m)^2 \times 10\,m \Rightarrow V = 480\,m^3$

12) Choice E is correct

Formula for the surface area of a cylinder is:

$SA = 2\pi r^2 + 2\pi rh \rightarrow 150\pi = 2\pi r^2 + 2\pi r(10) \rightarrow r^2 + 10r - 75 = 0$

Factor the expression and solve:

$r^2 + 10r - 75 = 0 \rightarrow (r + 15)(r - 5) = 0 \rightarrow r = 5 \; or \; r = -15 \; (unacceptable)$

13) Choice E is correct

The area of the circle is 16π, then, its diameter is 8.

Area of a circle $= \pi r^2 = 16\pi \rightarrow r^2 = 16 \rightarrow r = 4$

Radius of the circle is 4 and diameter is twice of it, 8.

One side of the square equals to the diameter of the circle. Then:

Area of square $= side \times side = 8 \times 8 = 64$

14) Choice A is correct

The median of a set of data is the value located in the middle of the data set. Combine the two sets provided, and organize them in increasing order:

$\{1, 3, 4, 6, 8, 10, 12, 14, 15, 17\}$

Since there are 10 numbers (an even number of items) in the resulting list, the median is the average of the two middle numbers. Median $= \frac{(8+10)}{2} = 9$

15) Choice C is correct

The area of the non-shaded region is equal to the area of the bigger rectangle subtracted by the area of smaller rectangle.

Area of the bigger rectangle $= 12 \times 16 = 192$

Area of the smaller rectangle $= 10 \times 4 = 40$

Area of the non-shaded region $= 192 - 40 = 152$

16) Choice E is correct

In the figure angle A is labeled $(3x - 2)$ and it measures 37. Thus, $3x - 2 = 37$ and $3x = 39$ or $x = 13$. That means that angle B, which is labeled $(5x)$, must measure $5 \times 13 = 65$.

Since the three angles of a triangle must add up to 180,

$37 + 65 + y - 8 = 180$, then: $y + 94 = 108 \rightarrow y = 180 - 94 = 86$

17) Choice D is correct

Let's find the mean (average), mode and median of the number of cities for each type of pollution. Number of cities for each type of pollution: $6, 3, 4, 9, 8$

$average \ (mean) = \frac{sum \ of \ terms}{number \ of \ terms} = \frac{6+3+4+9+8}{5} = \frac{30}{5} = 6$

The Median is the number in the middle. To find median, first list numbers in order from smallest to largest. $3, 4, 6, 8, 9$. The median of the data is 6.

Mode is the number which appears most often in a set of numbers. Therefore, there is no mode in the set of numbers. Median = Mean, then, $a = c$

18) Choice A is correct

Percent of cities in the type of pollution A: $\frac{6}{10} \times 100 = 60\%$

Percent of cities in the type of pollution C: $\frac{4}{10} \times 100 = 40\%$

Percent of cities in the type of pollution D: $\frac{9}{10} \times 100 = 90\%$

19) Choice A is correct

Let the number of cities should be added to type of pollutions B be x. Then:

$\dfrac{x+3}{8} = 0.625 \rightarrow x + 3 = 8 \times 0.625 \rightarrow x + 3 = 5 \rightarrow x = 2$

20) Choice E is correct

Let x be total number of cards in the box, then number of red cards is: $x - 246$

The probability of choosing a red card is one third. Then: $probability = \dfrac{1}{3} = \dfrac{x-246}{x}$

Use cross multiplication to solve for x.

$x \times 1 = 3(x - 246) \rightarrow x = 3x - 738 \rightarrow 2x = 738 \rightarrow x = 369$

21) Choice C is correct

Subtract $\dfrac{1}{6b}$ and $\dfrac{1}{b^2}$ from both sides of the equation. Then:

$\dfrac{1}{6b^2} + \dfrac{1}{6b} = \dfrac{1}{b^2} \rightarrow \dfrac{1}{6b^2} - \dfrac{1}{b^2} = -\dfrac{1}{6b}$

Multiply both numerator and denominator of the fraction $\dfrac{1}{b^2}$ by 6. Then:

$\dfrac{1}{6b^2} - \dfrac{6}{6b^2} = -\dfrac{1}{6b}$

Simplify the first side of the equation: $-\dfrac{5}{6b^2} = -\dfrac{1}{6b}$

Use cross multiplication method: $30b = 6b^2 \rightarrow 30 = 6b \rightarrow b = 5$

22) Choice C is correct

y is the intersection of the three circles. Therefore, it must be odd (from circle A), negative (from circle B), and multiple of 5 (from circle C).

From the choices provided, only -5 is odd, negative and multiple of 5.

23) Choice D is correct

Solve for x. $-2 \leq 2x - 4 < 2 \Rightarrow$ Add 4 to all sides: $-2 + 4 \leq 2x - 4 + 4 < 2 + 4 \Rightarrow$

$2 \leq 2x < 6$. Divide all sides by 2: $1 \leq x < 3$, Choice D represent this inequality.

24) Choice B is correct

Recall that the formula for the average is: $Average = \dfrac{sum\ of\ data}{number\ of\ data}$

First, compute the total weight of all balls in the basket: $25\ g = \dfrac{total\ weight}{20\ balls}$

$total\ weight = 25\ g \times 20 \rightarrow total\ weight = 500\ g$.

Next, find the total weight of the 5 largest balls:

$40\ g = \dfrac{total\ weight}{5\ marbles} \rightarrow total\ weight = 40\ g \times 5 \rightarrow total\ weight = 200\ g$

The total weight of the heaviest balls is 200 g. Then, the total weight of the remaining 15 balls is 300 g : 500 g – 200 g = 300 g.

The average weight of the remaining balls: Average $= \frac{300\ g}{15\ marbles} = 20\ g$ per ball

25) Choice A is correct

In the stadium the ratio of home fans to visiting fans in a crowd is 5 : 7. Therefore, total number of fans must be divisible by 12 : 5 + 7 = 12.

Let's review the choices:

A. 12,324 → 12,324 ÷ 12 = 1,027

B. 42,326 → 42,326 ÷ 12 = 3,527.166

C. 44,566 → 44,566 ÷ 12 = 3,713.833

D. 66,812 → 66,812 ÷ 12 = 5,567.666

E. 69,752 → 69,752 ÷ 12 = 5,812.666

Only choice A when divided by 12 results a whole number.

26) Choice A is correct

The area of the square is 595.36. Therefore, the side of the square is square root of the area: $\sqrt{595.36} = 24.4$

Four times the side of the square is the perimeter: 4 × 24.4 = 97.6

27) Choice D is correct

Fist convert mixed numbers to fractions: $2\frac{2}{3} - 1\frac{5}{6} = 2\frac{4}{6} - 1\frac{5}{6} = \frac{16}{6} - \frac{11}{6} = \frac{5}{6}$

28) Choice E is correct

$x = \frac{1}{3}$ and $y = \frac{9}{21}$, substitute the values of x and y in the expression and simplify:

$\frac{1}{x} \div \frac{y}{3} \rightarrow \frac{1}{\frac{1}{3}} \div \frac{\frac{9}{21}}{3} \rightarrow \frac{1}{\frac{1}{3}} = 3$ and $\frac{\frac{9}{21}}{3} = \frac{9}{63} = \frac{1}{7}$. Then: $\frac{1}{\frac{1}{3}} \div \frac{\frac{9}{21}}{3} = 3 \div \frac{1}{7} = 3 \times 7 = 21$

29) Choice E is correct

Let x be the number of current stamps in the collection. Then:

$\frac{6}{5}x - x = 100 \rightarrow \frac{1}{5}x = 100 \rightarrow x = 500$

50% more of 500 is: 500 + 0.50 × 500 = 500 + 250 = 750.

30) Choice C is correct

The sum of 8 numbers is greater than 240 and less than 320. Then, the average of the 8 numbers must be greater than 30 and less than 40.

$$\frac{240}{8} < x < \frac{320}{8} \rightarrow 30 < x < 40$$

The only choice that is between 30 and 40 is 35.

31) Choice B is correct

The angles on a straight line add up to 180 degrees. Then: $x + 25 + y + 2x + y = 180$

Then, $3x + 2y = 180 - 25 \rightarrow 3(35) + 2y = 155 \rightarrow 2y = 155 - 105 = 50 \rightarrow y = 25$

32) Choice B is correct

If two triangles are similar, then the ratios of corresponding sides are equal.

$$\frac{AC}{AE} = \frac{BC}{DE} = \frac{18}{9} = 2, \frac{AC}{AE} = 2$$

This ratio can be used to find the length of AC: $AC = 2 \times AE$, $AC = 2 \times 9 \rightarrow AC = 18$

The length of AE is given as 9 and we now know the length of AC is 18, therefore:

$EC = AC - AE, EC = 18 - 9, EC = 9$

33) Choice D is correct

Let E age of Ella, we know Ella is 4 years older than Ava: $E = 4 + A \rightarrow A = S - 3$

34) Choice C is correct

Let L be the length of the rectangular and W be the width of the rectangular. Then,

$L = 4W + 3$

The perimeter of the rectangle is 36 meters. Therefore: $2L + 2W = 36$, $L + W = 18$

Replace the value of L from the first equation into the second equation and solve for W: $(4W + 3) + W = 18 \rightarrow 5W + 3 = 18 \rightarrow 5W = 15 \rightarrow W = 3$

The width of the rectangle is 3 meters and its length is: $L = 4W + 3 = 4(3) + 3 = 15$

The area of the rectangle is: $Length \times Width = 3 \times 15 = 45$

35) Choice C is correct

The sum of two supplementary angles is 180 degrees. Then:

$(3x - 10) + (x + 2) = 180$. Simplify and solve for x: $(3x - 10) + (x + 2) = 180 \rightarrow$

$4x - 8 = 180 \rightarrow 4x = 180 + 8 \rightarrow 4x = 188 \rightarrow x = 47$

36) Choice E is correct

Let x be all expenses, then $\frac{22}{100}x = \$660 \to x = \frac{100 \times \$660}{22} = \$3,000$

He spent for his rent: $\frac{27}{100} \times \$3,000 = \$810$

37) Choice B is correct

To find the area of the shaded region subtract the area of the smaller circle from bigger circle.

$S_{bigger} - S_{smaller} = \pi(r_{bigger})^2 - \pi(r_{smaller})^2 \Rightarrow$

$S_{bigger} - S_{smaller} = \pi(6)^2 - \pi(4)^2 \Rightarrow 36\pi - 16\pi = 20\pi \ in^2$

38) Choice E is correct

The perimeter of the rectangle is: $2x + 2y = 30 \to x + y = 15 \to x = 15 - y$

The area of the rectangle is: $x \times y = 50 \to (15 - y)(y) = 50 \to y^2 - 15y + 50 = 0$

Solve the quadratic equation by factoring. $(y - 5)(y - 10) = 0 \to y = 5$ (Unacceptable, because y must be greater than 5) or $y = 10$

If $y = 10 \to x \times y = 50 \to x \times 10 = 50 \to x = 5$

39) Choice D is correct

First, find the measure of angle RQS. Angles RQS and PQR are supplementary and therefore their sum is 180 degrees. Then:

$PQR + RQS = 180 \to 135 + RQS = 180 \to RQS = 45$

The sum of all angles in a triangle is 180 degrees. Then:

$45 + 52 + x = 180 \to 97 + x = 180 \to x = 83$

40) Choice C is correct

x is directly proportional to the square of y. Then: $x = cy^2 \to 12 = c(2)^2 \to 12 = 4c \to$

$c = \frac{12}{4} = 3$. The relationship between x and y is: $x = 3y^2, x = 75 \to 75 = 3y^2 \to$

$y^2 = 25 \to y = 5$

41) Choice D is correct

The amount of money that Jack earns for one hour: $\frac{\$616}{44} = \$14$

A number of additional hours that he works to make enough money is: $\frac{\$826 - \$616}{1.5 \times \$14} = 10$

Number of total hours is: $44 + 10 = 54$

42) Choice E is correct

$2.5\% \ of \ 1200 = \frac{2.5}{100} \times 1200 = 30$

43) Choice D is correct

Solve for x: $x^3 + 18 = 130 \rightarrow x^3 = 112$

Let's review the choices.

A. 1 and 2 $1^3 = 1$ and $2^3 = 8$, 112 is not between these two numbers.

B. 2 and 3 $2^3 = 8$ and $3^3 = 27$, 112 is not between these two numbers.

C. 3 and 4 $3^3 = 27$ and $4^3 = 64$, 112 is not between these two numbers.

D. 4 and 5 $4^3 = 64$ and $5^3 = 125$, 112 is between these two numbers.

E. 5 and 6 $5^3 = 125$ and $6^3 = 126$, 112 is not between these two numbers.

44) Choice B is correct

15 second is one fourth of a minute. One fourth of 72 is 18. $72 \div 4 = 18$. Jack types 18 words in 15 seconds.

45) Choice E is correct

In scientific notation all numbers are written in the form of: $m \times 10^n$, where m is between 1 and 10. To find an equivalent value of 0.000,000,000,000,042,121, move the decimal point to the right so that you have a number that is between 1 and 10. Then: 4.2121. Now, determine how many places the decimal moved in step 1, then put it as the power of 10. We moved the decimal point 14 places. Then: 10^{-14} when the decimal moved to the right, the exponent is negative.

Then: $0.000,000,000,000,042,121 = 4.2121 \times 10^{-14}$

46) Choice C is correct

A. $|4 - 2| = |2| = 2$

B. $|2 - 4| = |-2| = 2$

C. $|-2 - 4| = |-6| = 6$

D. $|2 - 4| - |4 - 2| = |2| - |2| = 2 - 2 = 0$

E. $|2 - 4| + |4 - 2| = |-2| + |2| = 2 + 2 = 4$

Choice C is the largest number.

47) Choice C is correct

85% of 40 is: $0.85 \times 40 = 34$. So, the student solves 34 questions correctly.

48) Choice B is correct

Use simple interest formula:

$I = prt$ ($I = interest, p = principal, r = rate, t = time$)

Simple interest $I = 2,500 \times 0.08 \times 6 = 1,200$

She will pay \$1,200 interest at the end of 6 years.

49) Choice D is correct

The two greatest integers less than -3.34 are -4 and -5. Since -5 is odd, the answer is -4.

50) Choice C is correct

Since integer x is evenly divisible by 4, substitute 4 for x in the answer choices to determine which expression is also divisible by 4: Let $x = 4$.

Choice A:	$x + 1 = 4 + 1 = 5$	This is NOT divisible by 4.
Choice B:	$2x + 1 = 2(4) + 1 = 9$	This is NOT divisible by 4.
Choice C:	$2x + 4 = 2(4) + 4 = 12$	This is divisible by 4.
Choice D:	$3x + 2 = 3(4) + 2 = 14$	This is NOT divisible by 4.
Choice E:	$4x + 1 = 4(4) + 1 = 17$	This is NOT divisible by 4.

So, choice C is correct.

51) Choice E is correct

There are currently 16 balls in the bag $(5 + 8 + 3)$. Of those balls, 11 are not blue. So, the probability of choosing a ball that is not blue is $\frac{11}{16}$.

52) Choice B is correct

$ON = 4 - (-6) = 10$ units. Let $x = OM$. Then $MN = 10 - x$.

Substitute these expressions in the given equation: $x = \frac{1}{3}(10 - x)$

Solve for x: $x = \frac{10}{3} - \frac{x}{3} \rightarrow x + \frac{x}{3} = \frac{10}{3} \rightarrow \frac{4x}{3} = \frac{10}{3} \rightarrow 4x = 10 \rightarrow x = \frac{10}{4} = \frac{5}{2} = 2.5$

$x = OM$. Point O is at -6. Then, point M is at: $-6 + 2.5 = -3.5$

53) Choice D is correct

First, calculate Jack's riding time in minutes: 1 hour 20 minutes = 80 minutes

Then, convert kilometers to meters: 160 kilometers = 160,000 meters

Now simplify the ratio to find the answer: $\frac{160,000}{80} = 2,000$ meters

54) Choice E is correct

If x is the smaller consecutive integer, then $x + 1$ is the larger consecutive integer. Use their sum (-13) to find x:

$x + (x + 1) = -13 \rightarrow 2x + 1 = -13 \rightarrow 2x = -14 \rightarrow x = -7$

The two consecutive integers are -7 and -6. 2 is added to the smaller integer:

$-7 + 2 = -5$, and 3 is subtracted from the larger integer: $-6 - 3 = -9$ find the product: $-5 \times (-9) = 45$

55) Choice D is correct

The relationship among all sides of special right triangle

$30° - 60° - 90°$ is provided in this triangle:

In this triangle, the opposite side of 30° angle is half of the hypotenuse.

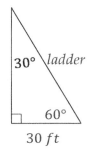

Draw the shape of this question:
The latter is the hypotenuse. Therefore, the latter is 60 ft

HiSET Mathematics Practice Test 2 explanations

1) Choice D is correct

The capacity of a red box is 20% bigger than the capacity of a blue box and it can hold 30 books. Therefore, we want to find a number that 20% bigger than that number is 30. Let x be that number. Then: $1.20 \times x = 30$. Divide both sides of the equation by 1.2. Then: $x = \frac{30}{1.20} = 25$

2) Choice C is correct

Convert everything into an equation: $35 = (3 \times \text{shirt}) - 10$

Now, solve the equation: $45 = 3\,\text{shirt} \rightarrow \text{shirt} = \frac{45}{3} = 15$. The price of the shirt was $15.

3) Choice E is correct

First, convert the improper fraction to a mixed number: $-\frac{32}{5} = -6\frac{2}{5}$

The two closest integers to this fraction are -7 and -6.

The integer less than $-\frac{32}{5}$ is -7.

4) Choice D is correct

Let x equal the smallest angle of the triangle. Then, the three angles are $x, 3x$, and $5x$. The sum of the angles of a triangle is 180. Set up an equation using this to find x:

$x + 3x + 5x = 180 \rightarrow 9x = 180 \rightarrow x = 20$

Since the question asks for the measure of the largest angle, $5x = 5(20) = 100°$

5) Choice E is correct

The angle $(2x - 5)$ and 55 are supplementary angles. Therefore:

$(2x - 5) + 55 = 180 \rightarrow 2x + 50 = 180 \rightarrow 2x = 180 - 50 \rightarrow 2x = 130 \rightarrow$

$x = \frac{130}{2} \rightarrow x = 65$

6) Choice A is correct

$average\ (mean) = \frac{sum\ of\ terms}{number\ of\ terms} \Rightarrow 85 = \frac{sum\ of\ terms}{50} \Rightarrow sum = 85 \times 50 = 4{,}250$

The difference of 94 and 69 is 25. Therefore, 25 should be subtracted from the sum.

$4{,}250 - 25 = 4{,}225, mean = \frac{sum\ of\ terms}{number\ of\ terms} \Rightarrow mean = \frac{4{,}225}{50} = 84.5$

7) Choice D is correct

Solve for x. $-4 \leq 4x - 8 < 16 \Rightarrow$ Add 8 to all sides: $-4 + 8 < 4x - 8 + 8 < 16 + 8 \Rightarrow$

$4 < 4x < 24 \Rightarrow$ Divide all sides by 4: $1 \leq x < 6$. Choice D represents this inequality.

8) Choice C is correct

Based on triangle similarity theorem: $\frac{a}{a+b} = \frac{c}{3} \rightarrow c = \frac{3a}{a+b} = \frac{3\sqrt{3}}{3\sqrt{3}} = 1 \rightarrow$ Area of shaded region is: $\left(\frac{c+3}{2}\right)(b) = \frac{4}{2} \times 2\sqrt{3} = 4\sqrt{3}$

9) Choice C is correct

A linear equation is a relationship between two variables, x and y, and can be written in the form of $y = mx + b$. A non-proportional linear relationship takes on the form $y = mx + b$, where $b \neq 0$ and its graph is a line that does not cross through the origin. Only in graph C, the line does not pass through the origin.

10) Choice D is correct

Based on triangle similarity theorem, set up a proportion to solve for x:

$\frac{x+8}{x} = \frac{6}{4} \rightarrow 4(x+8) = 6x \rightarrow 4x + 32 = 6x \rightarrow 32 = 2x \rightarrow x = 16$

11) Choice B is correct

Use simple interest formula:

$I = prt$ $(I = interest, p = principal, r = rate, t = time)$

$I = prt \rightarrow 600 = (3,000)(0.05)(t) \rightarrow 600 = 150t \rightarrow t = 4$

12) Choice D is correct

To solve, add the two given fractions: $2\frac{2}{5} + 1\frac{3}{4}$

The common denominator is 20: $2\frac{8}{20} + 1\frac{15}{20} = 3\frac{23}{20} = 4\frac{3}{20}$

13) Choice D is correct

Consider the case where $k = 1$

$n - k = 46 \rightarrow n - 1 = 46 \rightarrow n - 1 + 1 = 46 + 1 \rightarrow n = 47$

The list of integers from 1 to 47 contains 47 numbers.

14) Choice E is correct

The original piece of paper is $2\frac{3}{5}$ feet long.

The shorter piece is x feet long, and it must be less than half the length of the original piece of paper. Since half of $2\frac{3}{5}$ is $1\frac{3}{10}$ it follows that $x < 1\frac{3}{10}$.

15) Choice A is correct

First, find the sum of course grade of Anna, $average = \frac{sum\ of\ terms}{number\ of\ terms} \Rightarrow$

$80 = \frac{sum\ of\ course\ grade}{5} \rightarrow the\ sum\ of\ course\ grade = 80 \times 5 = 400$

Anna and William have the same sum of course grade, now find the Williams mean

$$average = \frac{sum\ of\ course\ grade}{number\ of\ course} \Rightarrow \frac{400}{8} = 50$$

16) Choice C is correct

Since both ratios have y in common, solve for x and z in terms of y in both equations. Using $x:y = 1:3$, solve for x in terms of y. $\frac{x}{y} = \frac{1}{3} \to x = \frac{1}{3}y$

Using the ratio $y:z = 2:5$, solve for z in terms of y: $\frac{y}{z} = \frac{2}{5} \to z = \frac{5}{2}y$

The question states $x + y + z = 69$

Substitute from the two equations above and solve for y.

$\frac{1}{3}y + y + \frac{5}{2}y = 69 \to \frac{2y+6y+15y}{6} = 69 \to \frac{23}{6}y = 69 \to 23y = 414 \to y = 18$

17) Choice D is correct

Multiply each term by 3 to eliminate the fraction, and isolate x:

$-1(3) < \left(\frac{x}{3}\right)(3) < 2(3) \to -3 < x < 6$, therefore, x must be between -3 and 6. Only Choice D represents all values of x.

18) Choice D is correct

List in order the odd numbers between 5 to 30: 7,9,11,13,15,17,19,21,23,25,27, and 29. Since, the numbers are consecutive odd numbers, the mean and the median are equal. The median is the number in the middle. Since we have 12 numbers, the median is the average of numbers 6 and 7 which are 17 and 19. The mean (or the median) is: Mean $= \frac{17+19}{2} = 18$

19) Choice C is correct

Square both sides of the equation: $(\sqrt{2y})^2 = (\sqrt{5x})^2 \to 2y = 5x$

Solve for x: $x = \frac{2}{5}y$

20) Choice B is correct

The area of a trapezoid can be determined using the formula: $A = \frac{1}{2} \times (a + b) \times h$

We know: $DC = 4\ cm$, $AE = 2\ cm$, and $AD = 4\ cm \to$

$A = \frac{1}{2} \times (4\ cm + 2\ cm) \times 4\ cm = 12\ cm^2$

21) Choice B is correct

60% of students can't swim$\to 100 - 60 = 40\%$ can swim.

Then: $0.40 \times 45 = 18$

22) Choice D is correct

Money received by 14 person = $8,400. So, the money received by one person is:
$\frac{\$8,400}{14} = \$600$

23) Choice A is correct

There are 12 sticks in the box (6 + 4 + 2). So, the probability that Emma picks a green stick is: $Probability = \frac{6}{12} = \frac{1}{2}$

24) Choice D is correct

First, calculate the area of the circle and the area of the square:

Area of the circle $= \pi r^2 = \pi(6)^2 = 36\pi = 113.04 \; cm^2$

Area of the square $= 5 \; cm \times 5 \; cm = 25 \; cm^2$

To calculate the shaded area, subtract the area of the square from the area of the circle: $113.04 \; cm^2 - 25 \; cm^2 = 88.04 \; cm^2$

25) Choice B is correct

Use the percent increase expression to find the answer:
$\frac{new \; price - original \; price}{original \; price} = \frac{5.67 - 5.40}{5.40} = 0.05 = 5\%$

26) Choice C is correct

Let x be the number of blue marbles. Write the items in the ratio as a fraction:

$\frac{x}{150} = \frac{4}{3} \rightarrow 3x = 600 \rightarrow x = 200$

27) Choice A is correct

Let x be the number: $\frac{5}{8}x = 90 \rightarrow x = 90 \times \frac{8}{5} = \frac{720}{5} = 144$

28) Choice E is correct

Set up a proportion to solve: $\frac{\frac{5}{14} \; cherry}{\frac{5}{70} \; apple} = \frac{x \; cherry}{1 \; apple} \rightarrow \frac{5}{14} \times \frac{70}{5} = x \rightarrow x = \frac{70}{14} = \frac{10}{2} \rightarrow x = 5$

29) Choice B is correct

The area of square $LMNO$ is 16 square centimeters.

So: $S^2 = 16 \rightarrow \sqrt{S^2} = \sqrt{16} \rightarrow S = 4 \; cm$

Sides LO and NO are each a radius of the circle. So, the radius of the circle is $4 \; cm$.

calculate the area of $\frac{1}{4}$ of the circle. The area of a circle is $A = \pi r^2$. So the area of the $\frac{1}{4}$ of the circle, in square centimeters, is $\frac{1}{4}A = \frac{1}{4}\pi r^2 = \frac{1}{4}\pi(4)^2 = \frac{1}{4}\pi(16) = 4\pi$. For calculating the area of shaded region, subtract area of $\frac{1}{4}$ of the circle from area of square. The area of the shaded par: $16 - 4\pi$: and $\pi = 3.14$, then, the answer is:

$16 - 4\pi = 16 - 12.56 = 3.44$

30) Choice D is correct

$2m = n + 5 \rightarrow m = \frac{n+5}{2}$. Substitute each value of n to find the values of m:

$$m = \frac{5+5}{2} = \frac{10}{2} = 5$$

$$m = \frac{3+5}{2} = \frac{8}{2} = 4$$

$$m = \frac{7+5}{2} = \frac{12}{2} = 6$$

The set of m is $\{5,4,6\}$

31) Choice B is correct

Plug in 25 for x in the equation.

A. $x + 10 = 40 \rightarrow 25 + 10 \neq 40$

B. $4x = 100 \rightarrow 4(25) = 100$

C. $3x = 70 \rightarrow 3(25) \neq 70$

D. $\frac{x}{2} = 12 \rightarrow \frac{25}{2} \neq 12$

E. $\frac{x}{3} = 8 \rightarrow \frac{25}{3} \neq 8$

Only choice B is correct.

32) Choice D is correct

Jack scored a mean of 80 per test. In the first 4 tests, the sum of scores is:

$80 \times 4 = 320$. Now, calculate the mean over the 5 tests: $\frac{320+90}{5} = \frac{410}{5} = 82$

33) Choice B is correct

Volume of the cube is less than $64 \ m^3$. Use the formula of volume of cubes.

Volume $= (one \ side)^3 \Rightarrow 64 = (one \ side)^3$. Find the cube root of both sides.

$64 = (one \ side)^3 \rightarrow one \ side = \sqrt[3]{64} = 4 \ m$

Then: $4 =$ one side. The side of the cube is less than 4. Only choice A is less than 4.

34) Choice C is correct

First draw an isosceles triangle. Remember that two legs of the triangle are equal.

Let put a for the legs. Then:

$a = 6 \Rightarrow$ Area of the triangle is $= \frac{1}{2}(6 \times 6) = \frac{36}{2} = 18 \ cm^2$

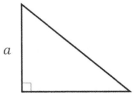

35) Choice C is correct

Solve for x: $0.00104 = \frac{104}{x}$, multiply both sides by x, $(0.00104)(x) = \frac{104}{x}(x)$.

Simplify: $0.00104x = 104$. Divide both side by 0.00104: $\frac{0.00104x}{0.00104} = \frac{104}{0.00104}$, simplify

$x = \frac{104}{0.00104} = 100,000$

36) Choice E is correct

The number of cards in the bag is 15.

$Probability = \frac{number \ of \ desired \ outcomes}{number \ of \ total \ outcomes} = \frac{1}{15}$

37) Choice D is correct

The equation of a line is in the form of $y = mx + b$, where m is the slope of the line and b is the $y - intercept$ of the line. Two points $(4,3)$ and $(3,2)$ are on line A. Therefore, the slope of the line A is: $m = \frac{y_2 - y_1}{x_2 - x_1} = \frac{2-3}{3-4} = \frac{-1}{-1} = 1$

The slope of line A is 1. Thus, the formula of the line A is: $y = x + b$, choose a point and plug in the values of x and y in the equation to solve for b. Let's choose point $(4, 3)$. Then:

$y = x + b \rightarrow 3 = 4 + b \rightarrow b = 3 - 4 = -1$

The equation of line A is: $y = x - 1$

Now, let's review the choices provided:

A. $(5, 7)$ $y = x - 1 \rightarrow 7 = 5 - 1 = 4$ This is not true.

B. $(3, 4)$ $y = x - 1 \rightarrow 4 = 3 - 1 = 2$ This is not true.

C. $(-1, 2)$ $y = x - 1 \rightarrow 2 = -1 - 1 = -2$ This is not true.

D. $(-1, -2)$ $y = x - 1 \rightarrow -2 = -1 - 1 = -2$ This is true.

E. $(-7, -9)$ $y = x - 1 \rightarrow -9 = -7 - 1 = -8$ This is not true.

38) Choice E is correct

$g(x) = -2$, then $f\big(g(x)\big) = f(-2) = 2(-2)^3 + 5(-2)^2 + 2(-2) = -16 + 20 - 4 = 0$

39) Choice B is correct

$(2x + 4)°$ and $96°$ are vertical angles. Vertical angles are equal in measure.

Then: $2x + 4 = 96 \rightarrow 2x = 92 \rightarrow x = 46$

40) Choice B is correct

The two-digit numbers must be even, so the only possible two-digit numbers must end in 6, since 6 is the only even digit given in the problem. Since the numbers cannot be repeated, the only possibilities for two-digit even numbers are 76 and 56. Thus, the answer is two possible two-digit numbers.

41) Choice A is correct

First convert 24 inches to feet. 12 inch = 1 feet, thus: $24 \div 12 = 2\ feet$. Then, calculate the volume, in cubic feet: $25 \times 6 \times 2 = 300\ ft^3$

42) Choice C is correct

Use properties of equations to determine the missing expression. $\frac{2y}{x} - \frac{y}{3x} = \frac{(\dots)}{3x}$

$\frac{3}{3} \cdot \frac{2y}{x} - \frac{y}{3x} = \frac{(\dots)}{3x} \rightarrow \frac{6y}{3x} - \frac{y}{3x} = \frac{(\dots)}{3x} \rightarrow \frac{6y - y}{3x} = \frac{(\dots)}{3x} \rightarrow (\dots) = 5y$

43) Choice D is correct

First calculate exponents value, then multiplying and subtracting:

$200(3 + 0.01)^2 - 200 = 200(3.01)^2 - 200 = 200(9.06) - 200 = 1,612.02$

44) Choice C is correct

Since 90 boxes contain $360\ kg$ vegetable. Therefore, 1 box contains $\frac{360\ kg}{90} = 4\ kg$ vegetable.

45) Choice C is correct

Let n represent a number in the sequence, and let x represent the number that comes just before n. $n = 4 + 2x \rightarrow 84 = 4 + 2x \rightarrow 80 = 2x \rightarrow x = 40$

46) Choice C is correct

Use PEMDAS (order of operation):$[6 \times (-24) + 8] - (-4) + [4 \times 5] \div 2 =$

$[-144 + 8] - (-4) + [20] \div 2 = [-144 + 8] + 4 + 10 = [-136] + 4 + 10 = -122$

47) Choice C is correct

First, find a common denominator for 2 and $\frac{3x}{x-5}$. It's $x - 5$. Then:

$2 + \frac{3x}{x-5} = \frac{2(x-5)}{x-5} + \frac{3x}{x-5} = \frac{2x-10+3x}{x-5} = \frac{5x-10}{x-5}$. Now, multiply the numerator and denominator of $\frac{3}{5-x}$ by -1. Then: $\frac{3 \times (-1)}{(5-x) \times (-1)} = \frac{-3}{x-5}$. Rewrite the expression: $\frac{5x-10}{x-5} = \frac{-3}{x-5}$. Since the denominators of both fractions are equal, then, the numerators must be equal.

$5x - 10 = -3 \rightarrow 5x = 7 \rightarrow x = \frac{7}{5}$.

48) Choice B is correct

Perimeter of rectangle is equal to the sum of all the sides of the rectangle:

Perimeter $= 2(14) + 2(5) = 28 + 10 = 38 \ cm$

49) Choice D is correct

$3\frac{1}{4} + 2\frac{4}{16} + 1\frac{3}{8} + 5\frac{1}{2}$. Convert all the fractions to a common denominator (16):

$3\frac{4}{16} + 2\frac{4}{16} + 1\frac{6}{16} + 5\frac{8}{16} = (3 + 2 + 1 + 5) + \left(\frac{4+4+6+8}{16}\right) = 11 + 1\frac{6}{16} = 12\frac{6}{16} = 12\frac{3}{8}$

50) Choice A is correct

One gram is equal to 1,000 milligrams, or 1 milligram is equal to $\frac{1}{1,000}$ gram.

Thus, 85 milligrams $= \frac{85}{1,000} = 0.085$ gram

51) Choice E is correct

Check each choice provided:

A. 1 $\frac{4+5+8+11+12}{5} = \frac{40}{5} = 8$

B. 4 $\frac{1+5+8+11+12}{5} = \frac{37}{5} = 7.4$

C. 5 $\frac{1+4+8+11+12}{5} = \frac{36}{5} = 7.2$

D. 8 $\frac{1+4+5+11+12}{5} = \frac{43}{5} = 8.6$

E. 11 $\frac{1+4+5+8+12}{5} = \frac{30}{5} = 6$

52) Choice E is correct

Substitute 6 for m and -3 for n:

$\frac{5-9(3+n)}{3m-5(2-n)} = \frac{5-9(3+(-3))}{3(6)-5(2-(-3))} = \frac{5-9(0)}{18-5(5)} = \frac{5}{18-25} = \frac{5}{-7} = -\frac{5}{7}$

53) Choice B is correct

To answer this question, we need to divide 28 by 7: $\frac{28}{7} = 4$

54) Choice B is correct

Simple interest (y) is calculated by multiplying the initial deposit (p), by the interest rate (r), and time (t). $360 = 240 \times 0.10 \times t \rightarrow 360 = 24t \rightarrow t = \frac{360}{24} = 15$

So, it takes 15 years to get \$360 with an investment of \$240.

55) Choice C is correct

There are 60 minutes in 1 hours. Divide the number of minutes by the number of minutes in 1 hour: $\frac{1,800}{60} = 30$ hours

Receive the PDF version of this book or get another FREE book!

Thank you for using our Book!

Do you LOVE this book?

Then, you can get the PDF version of this book or another book absolutely FREE!

Please email us at:

info@EffortlessMath.com

for details.

Author's Final Note

I hope you enjoyed reading this book. You've made it through the book! Great job!

First of all, thank you for purchasing this study guide. I know you could have picked any number of books to help you prepare for your HiSET Math test, but you picked this book and for that I am extremely grateful.

It took me years to write this study guide for the HiSET Math because I wanted to prepare a comprehensive HiSET Math study guide to help test takers make the most effective use of their valuable time while preparing for the test.

After teaching and tutoring math courses for over a decade, I've gathered my personal notes and lessons to develop this study guide. It is my greatest hope that the lessons in this book could help you prepare for your test successfully.

If you have any questions, please contact me at reza@effortlessmath.com and I will be glad to assist. Your feedback will help me to greatly improve the quality of my books in the future and make this book even better. Furthermore, I expect that I have made a few minor errors somewhere in this study guide. If you think this to be the case, please let me know so I can fix the issue as soon as possible.

If you enjoyed this book and found some benefit in reading this, I'd like to hear from you and hope that you could take a quick minute to post a review on the book's Amazon page. To leave your valuable feedback, please visit: amzn.to/3baKbTv

Or scan this QR code.

I personally go over every single review, to make sure my books really are reaching out and helping students and test takers. Please help me help HiSET Math test takers, by leaving a review!

I wish you all the best in your future success!

Reza Nazari

Math teacher and author

Made in the USA
Monee, IL
21 April 2022